Thomas Whittaker

Counsel and comfort for daily life

Thomas Whittaker

Counsel and comfort for daily life

ISBN/EAN: 9783337268978

Printed in Europe, USA, Canada, Australia, Japan

Cover: Foto ©Lupo / pixelio.de

More available books at **www.hansebooks.com**

COUNSEL AND COMFORT

FOR

DAILY LIFE

"Speak Lord, for thy servant heareth."
"Speak therefore unto me for the comfort of my soul, and to the amendment of my whole life, and to thy praise, and glory, and honor everlasting.

PUBLISHED BY
THE PROTESTANT EPISCOPAL SOCIETY FOR THE PROMOTION OF EVANGELICAL KNOWLEDGE,
No. 2 BIBLE HOUSE, FOURTH AVENUE, NEW-YORK.

PREFACE.

This little book is simply a collection of religious thoughts that have been gathered from many sources during the last few years, and published in the PARISH VISITOR. The desire of extending their influence has induced their republication in a more convenient and permanent form. To many the selections will be new. By others they will be welcomed as old friends that, from time to time, have helped them on their way.

These thoughts are again sent forth for the counsel and comfort of Christ's people, with the earnest prayer that through the Divine blessing on their silent ministry, many may be strengthened and refreshed in their daily life.

COUNSEL AND COMFORT
FOR DAILY LIFE.

THE KNOWLEDGE OF GOD.

THE knowledge of God is gained, as the knowledge of man is gained, by living much with Him. If we only come across a man occasionally, and in public, and see nothing of him in his private and domestic life, we cannot be said to know him. All the knowledge of God which many professing Christians have, is derived from a formal salute which they make to Him in their prayers, when they rise up in the morning, and lie down at night. While this state of things lasts, no great progress in the Christian life can possibly be made.

No progress *would* be made, even if they were to offer stated prayer seven times a day, instead of twice. But try to draw down God into your daily work; consult Him about it; offer it to Him as a contribution to His service; ask Him to help you in it; do it as to the Lord and not unto men; refer to Him in your temptations; seek a refuge under the shadow of His wings until the tyranny of temptation be overpast; go back *at once* to His bosom, when you are conscious of a departure from Him, not waiting till night to confess it, lest meanwhile the night of death should overtake you, or at best you should lose time in your spiritual course; in short, walk hand in hand with God through life (as a little child walks hand in hand with its father over some dangerous and thorny road), dreading above all things to quit His side, and assured that, as soon as you do so, you will fall into mischief and trouble. Seek not so much to pray, as to live in an *atmosphere* of prayer, lifting up your heart momentarily to Him in varied expressions of devotion, as the various occasions of life may prompt, adoring Him, thanking Him, resigning your will to Him many times a day, and more or less all day; and you shall thus, as you advance in this practice, as it becomes more and more habitual to you, increase in that knowledge of God which fully contents and satisfies the soul.

O GOD! MY HEART IS FIXED!

My whole desire
Doth deeply turn away
Out of all time, unto eternal day.
I give myself, and all I call my own,
To Christ forever, to be His alone.

I leave the world,
Its wealth allures not me :
With God alone, will I contented be.

The creature shall no longer fill my mind ;
In the Creator, what I want I find.

Now, O my God !
My comfort, portion, rest !
Thou, none but Thou, shalt reign within my breast.
Call me to Thee ! call me Thyself—oh ! speak,
And bind my heart to Thee, whom most I seek !

Then let me dwell
But as a pilgrim here :
One to whom earth seems distant—heaven more near.
Let this my joy, my life, my life-work be,
To die to self—to live, my Lord, to Thee.

I know this road
Through narrow straits doth wend,
Wherein my stubborn will must stoop and bend.
Jesus, I offer unto Thee my will—
Thy love can make it humble, sweet and still.

Thou art my King—
My King henceforth alone ;
And I Thy servant, Lord, am all Thine own.
Give me Thy strength : oh ! let Thy dwelling be
In this poor heart that pants, my Lord, for Thee.

WAITING IN FAITH.

You pray for some grace; you are answered by a temptation for which this grace is peculiarly needed. Is not *this* a swift answer to prayer, that you may learn at once the hopelessness of self-effort, and cast yourself on Him who says: "Call upon Me and I will answer thee, and show thee great and mighty things that thou knowest not"?

You desire some gift. Are you fitted for it? Were the Israelites prepared to enter the promised land as soon as they had passed the Red Sea? The spiritual blessing may seem near, almost realized, and then by some strange winding of our course be farther off than ever. Discouraged, we cry: "Hath God forgotten to be gracious? Hath He in anger shut up His tender mercies?" Nay, "If thou criest after knowledge, and liftest up thy voice for understanding; if thou seekest her as silver, and searchest for her as for hid treasures; then shalt thou understand the fear of the Lord, and find the knowledge of God." Such gifts are not received in some sudden effusion of the Spirit, but by means which often make us think our failures are greater, as morning light will disclose much that twilight conceals.

Be of good courage! God will have regard to the work of His own hands. With joy He hears you plead. If the natural prayer is often denied for blessing, the prayer for grace, is for God's glory; it is indicted by the Holy Spirit; it must be answered; it is the will of God. Though it tarry, wait for it.

WHEREIN WE HAVE PEACE.

SEE the simplicity of the ground on which your peace is to rest. God is well pleased in the finished work of Christ, " well pleased for His righteousness' sake." That righteousness is not founded upon your *feelings* or *experience*, but upon the shed blood of the Lamb of God, and hence your peace is not dependent upon your feelings or experience, but upon the precious blood which is of changeless efficacy and changeless value in the judgment of God.

"HAVING NOTHING."

Source of all good to which I aspire,
    Saviour most kind,
This is my hope and only desire,
    Thy favor to find.

My weakness and sin, my weariness, Lord,
    Are known unto Thee;
From heaven, whence all Thy bounties are poured,
    My want Thou dost see.

Thou knowest what good my spirit doth need
    All others above,
And how I am poor in all things, indeed,
    But most in Thy love.

Poor, wretched, and needy, I lie at Thy feet,
    Beseeching Thy grace ;
And wait, though unworthy, for what I entreat,
    A sight of Thy face.

Look down on a heart which only doth seek
    By Thee to be fed—
Which weary, and hungry, and guilty, and weak,
    Asks heavenly bread.

These icicles melt by the light of Thy face,
    Which hang in my heart,
And fill my whole soul with the shinings of grace,
    Till darkness depart.

Be Thou the sole glory and Thou the chief good,
    My heart to control ;
And be Thou the daily and hourly food,
    To nourish my soul.

Become its rejoicing, its stronghold of love,
    Its aim and its end ;
Its glory on earth, and its glory above,
    O Jesus, my friend.

"HE MUST INCREASE, I MUST DECREASE."

It is the Lord's love to me I would see, not mine to Him. I want to look at Him till I am not. This will not be, when I find myself having more love to God, more holiness, but when I lose myself and see Him to be my wisdom, righteousness, sanctification, redemption.

OUR PORTION.

We do not half realize the strength of that expression in the Bible, "Rejoice in the Lord." It is not, Rejoice in your health; it is not, Rejoice in your prosperity; it is not Rejoice in your wealth; it is not, Rejoice in your honor, or in your influence, or in those gifts which are the sources of most of our joy—it is, "Rejoice in the *Lord*." We are strong in God. Most of us do not know our joy and our strength, and die without realizing them.

What a pitiful thing it would be to see a man live all his life a pauper, and to find out just after he was buried that he was heir to an immense estate, that, held in trust, was waiting for him! How sad it would be for a man to be the unknown heir of a vast property, and yet live his whole life in poverty, and die without knowing anything about it, or having a penny of it! And yet there are thousands who are doing this in regard to spiritual things. They are living all their life long with an immense estate close by them, and not knowing anything about it, they do not break through and take possession of it.

ALL THINGS ARE YOURS.

While toil and warfare urge us on our way,
   And heart is answering heart in sighs of pain,
Have we no words of strengthening joy to say—
   No songs for those who suffer but to reign?

Behold the paths of life are ours we see
    Our blest inheritance where'er we tread;
Sorrow and danger our security,
    And disappointment lifting up our head.

Kings unto God, we may not doubt our power,
    We may not languish when He says "Be strong"—
We must move on through every adverse hour,
    And take possession as we pass along.

Yes, all is for us—nothing shall withstand
    Our faithful, valiant, persevering claim;
The rod of God's Anointed in our hand,
    And our assurance His unchanging name.

We need no haste when He has said "Be still"—
    No peace when He has charged us to contend;
Only the fearless love to do His will,
    And to show forth His honor to the end.

Oh ye that faint and die, arise and live!
    Sing, ye that all things have a charge to bless!
If He is faithful who hath sworn to give,
    Then be ye also faithful and *possess*.

THE MORNING QUESTION.

OH! that every morning, waking in the presence of God, the salutation which the first ray of recovered light brought to us, could be, "Child of God, handmaid of the Lord, a forgiven and a consecrated being!" What alacrity it would give to our movements, what reality to our communion with God, what earnestness and sweetness to our intercourse with one another!

If every morning, if but one morning, the whole multitude of believers, the whole family on earth, would gather round the Father, and each ask, "Lord, what, *this day*, wouldst Thou have me to do?"—as one by one left the Royal Audience, each with a special communion, what a rich day that would be for the Church and the world! What broken hearts would be bound up! what feeble hands would be lifted up! what blind eyes would be opened! how many tears would be wiped away! how many burdens lightened! how many lost souls brought back! how many weary, "because of the way," would be sent "on their way rejoicing!"

"WHAT WILT THOU HAVE ME TO DO?"

Hast Thou, my Master, aught for me to do
    To honor Thee to-day?
Hast Thou a word of love to some poor soul
    That mine may say?
For, see this world that Thou hast made so fair,
    Within its heart is sad;
Thousands are lonely, thousands sigh and weep,
    But few are glad.

But which among them all is mine to-day?
    Oh! guide my willing feet
To some poor soul that, fainting on the way
    Needs counsel sweet;
Or into some sick-room, where I may speak
    With tenderness of Thee;
And, showing who and what Thou art, O Christ!
    Bid sorrow flee!

Or, unto one whose straits call not for words—
  To one in want—in need ;
Who wills not counsel, but would take from me
  A loving deed.
Surely, Thou hast some work for me to do ;
  Oh ! open Thou mine eyes,
To see how Thou wouldst have it done,
  And where it lies.

THE MINISTRY OF SORROW.

The day will come when the veil shall be taken away, and then shall we see clearly how all things have worked together for the good of those that love God. Not in the days of peace, of calm delight in the Lord's house, of sweet content in good works, in duties gladly done, have we grown strong in the faith as it is in Jesus; but in the times when all confidence in ourselves had vanished, when sin and temptation were wildest, and we had no other anchor or refuge but the "Rock of Ages;" when we turned away from the examination of our hearts with loathing, to Jesus, the Author and Finisher of our faith. And so shall we see that as in our spiritual things, our deficiencies and sins have filled us with repentance, and led us nearer to the feet of our Lord, so in our temporal things have we been dealt with by a wise and tender Father, who has measured out to us joy and sorrow, prosperity and adversity, as best we were able to bear it.

THE FAITH THAT MOVES MOUNTAINS.

THE faith that deviseth great things is the faith which is intimate with God, and in sympathy with His mind. The faith that attempts and accomplishes great things is the faith that goes straight to God in everything, and deals directly with Him, maintaining unbroken the peace of conscience springing from the knowledge of the great blood-shedding, and holding fast the fellowship which the reconciling blood enables us constantly to realize. It is this faith that does great things, for it is faith that never loses sight of God in any part of the work. It counts upon success simply because it knows that the work is God's, and that whatever He is trusted for, assuredly comes to pass. It does not trust to accomplish small things because they are small; nor does it despond as to the achieving great things because they are great. It looks not to the nature of the work, nor regards either its facilities or its difficulties; it looks alone to Him whose work it is: who never fails His workmen; who is ever at hand for strength and succor.

WHAT ALL MAY DO.

You know how often it is difficult to be wisely charitable, to do good without multiplying the sources of evil. You know that to give alms is nothing unless you give thought also, and that therefore it is written, not, "Blessed is he that *feedeth* the poor, but "Blessed is he that *considereth* the poor." And you know that a little thought and a little kindness, are often worth more than a great deal of money.

"BEING PERPLEXED."

It is better to go at once to Jesus with our difficulties. We are worried and perplexed. Why not tell Jesus first instead of running with our griefs to our friends? However willing they may be, they are often unable to help us. The Christian who has learned to lean on Jesus for counsel and comfort, has learned the secret of the Lord—"The peace that passeth understanding." If we lived in the spirit of the following simple lines, what a load of care would be taken from our hearts!

"Being perplexed, I say,
　　Lord, make it right!
　　Night is as day to Thee,
　　Darkness is light.
I am afraid to touch
Things that involve so much:
　　My trembling hand may shake,
　　My skilless hand may break;
　　Thine can make no mistake.

"Being in doubt, I say,
　　Lord, make it plain!
　　Which is the true, safe way?
　　Which would be vain?
I am not wise to know,
Nor sure of foot, to go.
　　My blind eyes cannot see
　　What is so clear to Thee.
　　Lord, make it clear to me."

SINS REMEMBERED NO MORE.

WOULD it have been possible for God to have chosen words to express more pointedly and more vividly the utter putting out of remembrance the sins of His people than in such terms of love as these?

"I have *blotted out*, as a thick cloud, thy transgressions, and, as a cloud, thy sins." Who could attempt to gather together again the particles of a cloud that had been all dispersed?

"Thou wilt cast all their sins into the depths of the sea." Who would think of looking for a lost thing in "the depths of the sea"? How perfectly it conveys the idea of something profoundly hidden out of sight!

"Blessed is he whose sin is *covered*." When God has put a covering, shall man dare to lift it off? Yet He has "*covered*" the sins of His pardoned ones.

"Thou hast cast all my sins behind Thy back," and therefore they are no more "in the light of Thy countenance;" Thou lookest on them no more.

"As far as the east is from the west, *so far* hath He removed our transgressions from us." He has literally put them, may we not say, *out of our reach?*

Yea, we may search for them, but "they shall not be found." God remembers them no more.

FULL REST IN JESUS.

Jesus is not only the Forgiver of sin, but also the Deliverer from its *power*. He that abideth in Him sinneth not: he is passed from death unto life. "The blood of Jesus Christ cleanseth from all sin."

This truth is strikingly illustrated in the following extract:

"The beautiful pebble lies by the roadside, where every passing wheel shall cast dust upon it. Often as it is cleansed by the showers of heaven, it must always be again soiled. But if some kind hand shall place it beneath the flowing stream, it is not only cleansed, but kept pure evermore by the eternal waters. The clouds of dust and defilement shall never penetrate that stream, and in its eternal waters, the pebble shall evermore reflect the rays of the sun which shines upon it. It is thus with the soul which, abiding in Christ, is by faith able to say, moment by moment, ' *The blood cleanseth.*' "

DESULTORY WORK.

During the waiting season, while God withholds active work from the believer, He often gives little services to do for Him; work that may happen one day, and not another—" here a little, and there a little "— and which is often left undone, just because it is desultory, and apparently so small in its results. Many, however, are now in heaven who would never have known the way there had it not been for the religious book lent by a neighbor; or the persuasive letter penned in a distant land; or the awakening sermon listened to at the entreaty of a Christian friend; or the tract found in a railway-station; or the short, sudden, but heaven-heard and heaven-answered prayer; or the timely-spoken word by the way-side; or the hymn lovingly taught to the little child; or the striking anecdote treasured up and repeated; or the pointed verse of scripture that went into the heart, sharpened as a two-edged sword.

The very crumbs of work that fall from the Master's hand—the fragments that remain from what He gives His strong ones, the "corners of time," snatched from the more secular work of every day—ought to be treasured by the Christian. They whose time is much at the disposal of others, or who are much in the habit of travelling from place to place, and therefore peculiarly fitted for a wayside witnessing for Christ, need to consider deeply the importance of seizing all opportunites for desultory work. How well it would be, if each, in going through the world, were to remember what the old writer said of life—that it consisted of two heaps, a large one of sorrow, and a small one of happiness, and whoever carried the very smallest atom from the one to the other, did God a service; much more those who are instrumental, in any way, in leading or helping one precious soul from the pit of eternal misery to the home of eternal joy.

"WAITING AND WATCHING FOR ME."

An old tradition says that those we have served on earth shall be the first to welcome us in heaven.

When mysterious whispers are floating around,
  And voices that will not be still,
Shall summon us hence from the slippery shore,
  To the waves that are silent and still—
When I look with changed eyes at the home of the
    blest,
  Far out of the reach of the sea,
Will any one stand at the beautiful gate,
  Waiting and watching for me?

There are dear ones at home I may bless with my love,
  There are wretched ones passing the street;
There are friendless and suffering strangers around,
  There are tempted and poor I must meet;
There are many unthought of, whom happy and blest,
  In the land of the good I shall see;
Will any of them, at the beautiful gate,
  Be waiting and watching for me?

There are old and forsaken, who linger awhile
  In the homes which their dearest have left,
And an action of love or a few gentle words
  Might cheer the sad spirit bereft.
But the Reaper is near to the long-standing corn,
  The weary shall soon be set free;
Will any of these, at the beautiful gate,
  Be waiting and watching for me?

There are little ones glancing about on my path,
　In need of a friend and a guide ;
There are dim little eyes looking up into mine,
　Whose tears could be easily dried ;
But Jesus may beckon the children away,
' In the midst of their grief or their glee ;
Will any of these, at the beautiful gate,
　Be waiting and watching for me ?

I may be brought there by the manifold grace
　Of the Saviour, who loves to forgive ;
Though I bless not the hungry ones near to my side,
　Only pray for myself while I live.
But I think I should mourn o'er my selfish neglect—
　If sorrow in heaven can be—
If no one should stand at the beautiful gate,
　Waiting and watching for me.

THE COVERING OF CHARITY.

St. Peter exhorts his brethren to cultivate love—love for one another. This love should be placed before all other virtues, and should be so fervent, so intense, and so comprehensive, as to give tone and character to the whole life. Such a love, he assures us, shall cover a multitude of sins. Not the sins of the individual who exercises it, but the sins of others. The Apostle would teach us that the spirit of true love, a Christian love, will incline us to look charitably upon the conduct of those around us. It will hide from view, throw a mantle, as it were, over the faults and failings of others, and thus cover them up. We are ready enough, perhaps, to look kindly upon those who stand very near to us. We are blind to their defects; or, if not quite so, we are very lenient, and are careful not to speak of them to others. Now, the Spirit of Christ bids us exercise the same thoughtful kindness toward everybody; not toward our family and friends alone, but toward all with whom we have to do. We ask our heavenly Father to look pityingly and tenderly upon ourselves and those we love, for we know we could not answer for one of a thousand of our offences. But how can we expect He will hear us, unless we are willing to exercise the same spirit toward our fellow-men? If God should deal with us as we deal with each other, who could stand?

Let us not deceive ourselves. It is not by discipline or self-control, not by silence or indifference, that we are to attain this end. This would be but a cold, a negative virtue. The Apostle tells us there must be love—fervent, heart-felt love; a love which inspires the deepest and liveliest interest in others. Such a love, he assures us, will cover up and hide from our view the frailties and infirmities, the errors and the sins of those around us. God give us this spirit!

ANXIOUS THOUGHT.

"Take no thought for the morrow;" its trials or
    dangers ;
Why burden thy spirit with deepening gloom?
Ah! to-day hath enough to distress and perplex thee,
    It needeth no shadow of dark things to come.

"Take no thought for the morrow." No sorrow shall
    touch thee
But that which thy God in His love hath decreed ;
Go to Christ with thy grief, as it daily ariseth,
    And seek for His strength in the moment of need.

"Take no thought for the morrow." Its dawning may
    find thee
A spirit at rest 'neath the altar of God :
With the last battle fought, and the last trial ended—
    The victory won through Emmanuel's blood.

HOPE FOR ALL.

Baxter says, "The good are not so good as I once thought, nor the bad so evil; and in all there is more for grace to make advantage of, and more to testify for God and holiness, than I once believed."

FORGETTING THE PAST.

It is wise to forget past errors. There is a kind of temperament which, when indulged, greatly hinders growth in real godliness. It is that rueful, repentant, self-accusing temper, which is always looking back, and microscopically observing how that which is done might have been better done. Something of this we ought to have. A Christian ought to feel always that he has partially failed; but that ought not to be the only feeling. Faith ought ever to be a sanguine, cheerful thing; and, perhaps, in practical life, we could not give a better account of faith than by saying that it is amidst much failure, having the heart to try again. Our best deeds are marked by imperfection; but if they really were our best,—"forget the things that are behind,"—we shall do better next time.

Under this head, we include all those

mistakes which belong to our circumstances. We can all look back to past life, and see mistakes that have been made—to a certain extent, perhaps, irreparable ones. The profession chosen for you, perhaps, was not the fittest; or you are out of place, and many things might have been better ordered. Now, on this apostolic principle, it is wise to forget all that. It is not by regretting what is irreparable, that true work is to be done, but by making the best of what we are. It is not by complaining that we have not the right tools, but by using well the tools we have. What we are, and where we are, is God's providential arrangement—God's doing, though it may be man's misdoing; and the manly and the wise way is to look your disadvantages in the face, and see what can be made out of them. Life, like war, is a series of mistakes; and he is not the best

Christian, or the best general, who makes the fewest false steps. Poor mediocrity may secure that; but he is best who wins the most splendid victories by the retrieval of mistakes. Forget mistakes; organize victory out of mistakes.

HARSH JUDGMENTS.

O God! whose thoughts are brightest lights,
    Whose love always runs clear,
To whose kind wisdom sinning souls
    Amidst their sins are dear!

Sweeten my bitter-thoughted heart
    With charity like Thine,
Till self shall be the only spot
    On earth which does not shine.

Time was, when I believed that wrong
    In others to detect
Was part of genius, and a gift
    To cherish, not reject.

Now, better taught by Thee, O Lord!
    This truth dawns on my mind—

The best effect of heaven'y light
  Is earth's false eyes to blind.

How Thou canst think so well of us,
  Yet be the God Thou art,
Is darkness to my intellect,
  But sunshine to my heart.

Yet habits linger in the soul!
  More grace, O Lord! more grace!
More sweetness from Thy loving heart!
  More sunshine from Thy face.

SUNDAY A DAY OF GLADNESS.

God does not mean us always to be sombre, least of all upon Sunday, the glad feast of the Resurrection, a day whose atmosphere throughout should be one of quiet, unworldly joy. Let not boisterous merriment disturb the calm; let hearty worship, and kindly intercourse, and refreshing rest—rest of tired mind from its dragging brood of week-day anxieties, rest of tired body from the round of week-day toil—let this be the employment, this the tone of the hallowed day. Religion, not in every word, act, look, obtruded with painful effort, but present in the heart, should pervade the day, its rest, its reading, its conversation. Oh! never represent Sunday — at any rate, to the young — as a dull and gloomy day; nor dream that a heart devoted to the kind God, need abjure all that is genial and joyous, or that a subdued, spirit-broken step is necessary to the child who has chosen to walk beside that tender Father, holding by His hand.

LOOKING UNTO JESUS.

SIN is never overcome by looking at it, but by looking away from it to Him who bore our sins, yours and mine, on the cross. The heart is never won back to God by thinking we ought to love Him, but by learning what He is—all worthy of our love.

MY SINS, AND MY SAVIOUR!

"My sins have taken such hold upon me that I am not able to look up; yea, they are more in number than the hairs of my head, and my heart hath failed me."

My sins, my sins, my Saviour!
   They take such hold on me,
I am not able to look up,
   Save only, Christ, to Thee;
In Thee is all forgiveness,
   In Thee abundant grace;
My shadow and my sunshine,
   The brightness of Thy face.

My sins, my sins, my Saviour!
   How sad on Thee they fall;
Seen through Thy gentle patience,
   I tenfold feel them all;
I know they are forgiven,
   But still their pain to me
Is all the grief and anguish,
   They laid, my Lord, on Thee.

My sins, my sins, my Saviour!
   Their guilt I never knew

Till with Thee in the desert
   I near Thy passion drew ;
Till with Thee in the garden
   I heard Thy pleading prayer,
And saw the sweat-drops bloody
   That told Thy sorrow there.

Therefore my songs, my Saviour,
   E'en in this time of woe,
Shall tell of all Thy goodness
   To suffering man below ;
Thy goodness and Thy favor,
   Whose presence from above,
Rejoice those hearts, my Saviour,
   That live in Thee, and love.

GREATLY AFFLICTED.

I HAVE felt that terrible calamities are great blessings to the spirit of a man who knows how to suffer. To such a man a great affliction from God is like a great blast in a quarry—it throws out great treasures, or it opens a way for great projects. I revere a man who is in great affliction.

God seems to have selected him, like a piece of second-growth timber, for an important work. It is not every one who can be trusted to suffer greatly.

WHITEFIELD'S PRAYER.

"If not in public usefulness, yet in heart-holiness, let thy servant grow, O Lord!" So prayed this devoted servant of God in a time of sickness. How heavenly a place must that sick-room have been! How useful those hours of weakness! For the believer's usefulness increases in proportion to his growth in holiness. God's light is never wasted. If the light is in your heart, it is in your life. It must shine. Make the most then of this season of retirement. It is your preparation for future usefulness. "Take comfort, afflicted Christian," writes an eminent divine; "you have often prayed to be made of some service in the world before you die, and now the answer to that prayer has come. God tries you because in some way He is about to use you; for your history will furnish no exception to the rule, that when God is about to make preëminent use of a man, He puts him in the fire."

To this end let it be your aim to grow in heart-holiness. And may the effects of these suffering days be, "that Christ shall dwell in your heart by faith; that, being rooted and grounded in love, you may be enabled to comprehend, with all saints, what is the breadth and length and depth and height, and to know the love of Christ, which passeth knowledge."

PROMPTNESS IN DUTY.

NEVER judge by appearances as to the relative importance of duties. What seems the least important may be all-important.

Had the widow not given her mite the day she did to the treasury, but delayed it a week, how much would she herself, and the whole Christian Church, have lost by the delay!

THE SUFFERER'S COUCH.

"Those members of the body which seem to be more feeble, are necessary."—1 Cor. xii. 22.

"My work is done—I lay me down to die:
   Weary and travel-worn, I long for rest.
Speak but the word, dear Master, and I fly,
   A dove let loose, to nestle on Thy breast."
"Not yet, my child; a little longer wait,
   I need thy prayerful watch at glory's gate."

"But, Lord, I have no strength to watch or pray;
   My spirit is benumbed, and dim my sight;
And I shall grieve Thy wakeful love, as they
   Who in the garden slept that Paschal night."
"My child, I need thy weakness, hour by hour,
   To prove, in Me, thy strengthlessness is power."

" Not for myself alone I urge the suit ;
   But loved ones lose for me life's printless bloom ;
And tender, patient, uncomplaining, mute,
   Wear out their joyance in my darkened room."
" Enough, my child ; I need their love to thee ;
   Around thy couch, they minister to Me."

" It is enough, dear Master—yea, amen ;
   I will not breathe one murmur of reply ;
Only fulfil Thy work in me, and then
   Call me, and bid me answer, 'Here am I!' "
" My child, the sign I waited for is given ;
   Thy work *is* done ; I need thee now in heaven."

A FORM OF UNBELIEF.

THE humble man, of course, invariably forms a very modest estimate of his own place and power; and the more graciously humble he is, the more modest will his self-estimate ever be. But out of this excellent spirit a dangerous temptation may arise. A man may fancy himself to be so insignificant, and his efforts to be so very worthless, that he and his influence are the smallest of trifles, and it shall matter little whether he attempt to do his appointed work or not. Take heed, my reader, of this mock humility. Your tempter may look like the brightest of the angels of light, but his real name is Unbelief, not Humility. What you feel in regard to yourself every Christian may equally feel in regard to his work; and if every Christian were to neglect his duties because he feels himself incompetent to discharge them, how shall Jacob ever be made to arise? No, no; cherish those modest thoughts of yourself, for they are all true; but dismiss your unworthy thoughts of Christ, for these are false. His power is such that, even with you He can accomplish anything. There is no duty to which you are really called, that you are not quite able to discharge, with Christ strengthening you. Whatever you may be,

God is "able to make all grace abound toward you, that ye, always having all sufficiency in all things, may abound to every good work." Your sense of impotence is rightly used when it sends you, in humble faith, to Christ for help; but you abuse it if you are led by it to bury your talents in the earth, and thereby to earn the slothful servant's doom. Throughout the whole economy of grace—in the service of the Christian as well as in the frank forgiveness of the sinner—grace is reigning; and God delights to employ the self-emptied little ones for the doing of His greatest works.

THE HEART OF UNBELIEF.

"Help Thou mine unbelief."—MARK xix. 24.

'Tis not the cross I have to bear,
'Tis not the cup of pain and care,
Which constitute my bitter grief:
It is the heart of unbelief!

The cross would be but light without
The boding fear—the anxious doubt;
And honey drops my cup would fill,
But for this rebel, restless will.

'Twas unbelief which sowed the thorn
By which these weary feet were torn :
'Tis unbelief and fear which hide
The pleasant brooks on either side.

'Tis faith which hails the fountain's flow
And sees the desert lily blow,
And listens patiently to hear
The blessed Master drawing near.

Dear Lord! from whom our hearts receive
The grace to hear Thee and believe,
Take from my cross its only grief,
And help, oh! help mine unbelief!

WORK FOR ALL.

GOD never put one man or woman into the world, without giving each something to do in it or for it—some visible, tangible work, to be left behind them when they die.

AS WE HAVE OPPORTUNITY.

"As we have therefore opportunity, let us do good unto all men." In doing good, our obligations are limited only by our opportunities. We make our mistakes in not recognizing them. One man always has the opportunity; another never seems to find it. And this makes the broad distinction between useful and useless persons. Two persons in the same neighborhood, and in similar circumstances, travel wide apart as they go on in life, because one improves his opportunities, the other does not. Had we the spirit of our Master, we should find life full of occasions for blessing others. There are always opportunities where there are willing hearts. The love that seeketh not her own, is quick to see the needs and sorrows of others. It is not want of work, but want of love that holds us back. It has been well said that "there is plenty of work wherever there are sin and sorrow, and there are sin and sorrow everywhere." In little things, we may do much every day. A simple expression of interest in the things of another; a readiness to enter heartily into the daily trials and perplexities, joys and sorrows of those around us, how much will this spirit add to the comfort and happiness of a household! Again, a cheerful, contented spirit carries sunshine everywhere. How it brightens every-day life, and blesses all within its reach! It does good "unto all men." Surely we *have* opportunity at all times, in all places. Let us see to it then that we have the willing mind— the mind that was in Christ Jesus.

EVIL SPEAKING.

"SPEAK evil of no man," says the great apostle; as plain a command as "Thou shalt do no murder." But who, even among Christians, regard this command?

What is evil-speaking? It is not the same as lying or slandering. All a man says may be as true as the Bible, and yet the saying of it be evil-speaking. For evil-speaking is neither more nor less than speaking evil of an absent person; relating something evil which was really done or said by one that is not present when it is related.

A PILLOW PRAYER.

The day is ended. Ere I sink to sleep,
  My weary spirit seeks repose in Thine;
Father! forgive my trespasses, and keep
    This little life of mine.

With loving-kindness curtain Thou my bed,
  And cool in rest my burning pilgrim feet:
Thy pardon be the pillow for my head—
    So shall my sleep be sweet.

At peace with all the world, dear Lord, and Thee;
No fears my soul's unwavering faith can shake;
All's well! whichever side the grave for me
The morning light may break!

COMING BACK TO CHRIST.

I FEEL, when I have sinned, an immediate reluctance to go to Christ—I am ashamed to go. I feel as if it would do no good to go—as if it were making Christ a minister of sin, to go straight from the swine, through to the best robe—and a thousand other excuses; but I am persuaded that they are all lies, direct from hell. John argues the opposite way. "If any man sin we have an Advocate with the Father," and a thousand other Scriptures are against it. I am sure there is neither peace, nor safety from deeper sin but in going directly to the Lord Jesus Christ. This is God's way of peace and holiness. It is folly to the world and the beclouded heart, but it is the way. I must never think sin too small to need immediate application to the blood of Christ. If I put away a good conscience concerning faith, I make shipwreck. I must think my sins too great, too aggravated, too presumptuous—as when done on my knees, or in preaching, or by a dying bed, or during dangerous illness—to hinder me from fleeing to Christ. The weight of my sins should act like the weight of a clock—the heavier it is, it makes it go the faster.

A PRECIOUS PROMISE.

"How much more shall your Heavenly Father give the Holy Spirit to them that ask Him."

THE Saviour had been teaching His disciples how to pray, and had illustrated the willingness of our Heavenly Father to give every needed blessing to those who asked

Him, by a comparison with an earthly parent's readiness to respond to all his children's wants, and then with an outburst of tender love and compassion He speaks the words we have quoted.

This has always been to us a most precious and comforting text, and sustained us in many a conflict, and lighted many a dark way along our pilgrimage.

In the midst of powerful temptations, when the struggle seems to be going against you, or when you are conscious that the world is gaining the mastery over you, or more than either, when some secret sin has been indulged, until it has separated between you and your God, and you know not how to break its spell, and yet know that it must be crushed; then plead this promise of God, and on this ground. You do not in this prayer ask for long life, or health, or prosperity, or even for happiness; no earthly, selfish motive mingles with it, but the sincere, often tearful, and sometimes heart-broken cry for deliverance from sin, its power and its consequences. It is an earnest appeal of a child that has wandered but still loves, of a heart that longs for deliverance and purity and peace; and when you take this promise, which will never seem so great and precious to you as when your soul is very weary of its sins, and plead it before your Father's throne as one pleads for his life, the Holy Spirit shall give you the victory over your sin, whatever may be its power, and the sweet peace of forgiveness shall fill your heart.

"I will heal their backsliding; I will love them freely, for mine anger is turned away."

CHRIST-LIKE.

NEVER address the vilest outcast as you would not speak to your dearest friend,

COMPLETE IN HIM.

Full of failings, now my soul
　Seeketh in the darkness light;
Jesus! hear Thou, show Thy face,
　Put the shadows all to flight;
I entreat Thee let me see Thee,
　Hide no longer in the night!

I perceive it; my rebellion
　Is the cause of all my grief;
I confess it, and beseech Thee
　For forgiveness and relief;
Thou canst give me, O my Jesus,
　Help, and grace, and new belief.

In the future let me serve Thee
　Wisely in Thy chosen way;
Ever truer, purer, brighter,
　Growing like Thee every day;
Men shall see that all my power
　Comes from Thee, whom I obey.

Teach me, lead me, and prepare me;
　As Thou wilt, my soul refine;
Let Thy love fill my desire,
　And through all my life-work shine.

O what blessing, O what glory,
    Thus to cry, Thou mine, I thine!

Jesus, keep me, till Thy presence
    Shineth out before my eyes,
Where Thy children weep no longer,
    Where are heard no bitter sighs.
Step by step I'll mount the ladder
    On which men to Thee may rise.

LIFE IN CHRIST.

I know not what should more cheer and gladden a Christian than to see his spiritual life losing everything of an exotic character; to have it set in the open air, welcoming the wind from every quarter; acquiescing in all things because depending only upon one. A free and sustained spirit becomes natural to him who in the breaking of his daily bread, has found that Real Presence which sanctifies and glorifies our life's poor Elements. When the heart has found its true gravitation, it leaves that Rest slowly and returns to it quickly; disturbing influences will be felt from time to time, but their power is gone. "*That which is the strongest must win.*"

A firm, assured patience grows upon the Christian, enabling him to hold upon his way undeterred, unchilled by whatever he may meet upon it; enabling him also, I know not to what inner music, to build up his spirit to a strength of calm, reliant conviction, even with the stones he finds there, as a brook lifts up a more clear and rapid voice, for flowing over pebbles. The strain upon the inner life has passed over from self to Christ. The heart has grown wiser, instructed, tolerant, tender with weakness, patient of imperfection.

How quiet such a life is! how fruitful! Fruitful because it is so quiet; it works not, but lives and grows. The uneasy effort has passed out of it; *unresting because it rests al-*

way, it has done with task-work and anxiety; it serves, yet it is not cumbered with much serving; it has ceased from that sad complaint, "Thou hast left me to serve alone."

Such a life will seem less spiritual only because it has grown more natural; the soul moves in an atmosphere which of itself brings it into contact with all great and enduring things, and it has only to draw in its breath to be filled and satisfied. I know not how to describe the grandeur and simplicity of the state that is no longer self-bounded, self-referring; how great a thing to such a freed and rejoicing spirit, the life in Christ Jesus seems; a temple truly "not of this building," too great to be perfect here; a thought for which our mortal life—a language as yet too broken and confused to "catch up the whole of love and utter it"— can find no corresponding word.

SING AWAY YOUR GRIEF.

We can sing away cares easier than we can reason them away.

Oh, that we could put songs under our burdens! Oh, that we could extract the sense of sorrow by song! Then these things would not poison so much. Sing in the house. Teach your children to sing. When troubles come, go at them with songs. When griefs arise, sing them down. Lift the voice of praise against cares. Praise God by singing; that will lift you above trials of every sort. Attempt it. They sing in heaven; and among God's people upon earth, song is the appropriate language of Christian feeling.

THE TRUE STANDARD.

Those that are bound for heaven must be willing to swim against the stream, and must not do as *most* do, but as the *best* do.

ALL IN THEE.

Weakness and trouble, solitude and sorrow,
  In combination! can I cheerful be?
And wherefore not, since I can voices borrow,
  Society and light and peace from Thee,
      My God, from Thee?

I will not waste one breath of life in sighing;
  For other ends has life been given to me;
Duties and self-devotion—daily dying
  Into a higher, better life with Thee,
      Dear Lord, with Thee!

Strong in Thy strength, though in myself but weakness,
  Equal to all, I know that I shall be,
If I can seize the mantle of Thy meekness
  And wrap it round my soul, like Thee,
      Blest Lord, like Thee!

JESUS THE HOME OF THE SOLITARY.

"My *mother*, and *sister*, and *brother* "—not a word ever fell from His lips which was not laden with meaning. What, then, can these words mean, but that there is not a relationship on earth the tenderness of which His love does not contain and exceed, and the want of which, He, in His own person, cannot freely supply?

There is not a vacant place in the heart or the home He cannot fill, nor an energy of the renewed affections which may not find its full exercise through Him. Personally, Jesus can be, and designs to be this to those who believe in Him. In the abundance of natural ties, in the fullest home, and the life richest in natural influence and necessary activity, the heart of the Christian can find rest in none but Christ; and in the most solitary life, in the emptiest home, though it be but the one hired room, where domestic plans and labors lose all their poetry and sweetness by becoming merely the necessary providing for self, those meals which in the family are such happy gatherings and focuses of family history, sinking into nothing more than the sustenance of the body, the love and the presence of Jesus can entirely satisfy the heart, and make it not only always content, but often in a glow of thankfulness, turning the solitary meal into a feast of gladness, and hallowing the solitary room with high and sweet associations. I believe not only that this is possible, but that it has been, and at this moment is, the case in many a home known but to God and the angels who minister there.

UNCONSCIOUS INFLUENCE.

Not more constantly is the sun pouring forth its beams, or a flower exhaling its fragrance, than the Christian is radiating or exhaling influence from his character upon those around him. Wherever he is, whatever he does, this influence never ceases. It underlies all his actions; it runs side by side with his words; it goes on when action ceases and words fail. What a man voluntarily chooses, says, or does, is only occasional. He does not always think or always act. From pure fatigue he must, perforce, be silent and inactive at times. But what he *is*—that is necessarily perpetual and coextensive with his being.

I cannot always speak a word for Christ, but I can always *live* for Him. I cannot always do good actively. I may not have the opportunity, though I have the inclination; but I can always *be* good, passively. The voluntary language of what I say or do, is spasmodic, and liable to continual interruption; but the language of my character, of what I really am, is as continuous as my life itself, and suffers no more interruption than the beating of my heart or the breathing of my lungs. I can choose to do good or evil, to say a kind or bitter word; but I cannot choose to exert or repress the influence of my character, for it acts in spite of me—it produces its own proper impression, whether I think of it or not. I cannot live at all without radiating this influence. "Simply to be in this world is to exert an influence compared with which mere words and acts are feeble." Just as the leaven, by its mere presence, changes the particles of meal in the midst of which it is hid, so does each human being, by his mere presence, affect for good or evil those with whom he associates.

A GIFT.

God's salvation is not a purchase to be made, nor wages to be earned, nor a summit to be climbed, nor a height to be attained, but simply and solely a gift to be received. And nothing but faith can receive anything from God.

THE SECRET SPRING.

"He shall be as a tree planted by the waters, and that spreadeth out her roots by the river, and shall not see when heat cometh, but her leaf shall be green."—Jer. xvii. 7, 8.

The gentle moon was silvering
   The outline of the trees,
The lullaby of Nature
   Was whispered in the breeze.
'Twas not a time for talking,
   Or speculations high :
I wanted to be quiet,
   And hear that lullaby

I wanted to be silent,
   And watch the waving grass,
So gracefully inclining
   To let the breezes pass.
It seemed to grow in beauty
   The more it bowed its head,
Like penitential murmurs
   On saintly dying bed.

I marvelled at its beauty,
   So manifold, so sweet,
Like rainbow colors blending
   In harmony complete.

FOR DAILY LIFE.

And while I looked, and wondered
    What made it grow so high,
The question rose within me,
    Is there a hid supply?

For it was taller, fairer
    Than all the grass around;
What made it thus to differ
    From cumberers of the ground?
At last, the whispering breezes
    This answer seemed to bring
(Its echoes rang within me),
    "There is a SECRET SPRING!

"You cannot see the waters
    By which the grass is fed;
You cannot see the brooklet,
    Within its little bed;
You cannot even hear it,
    So quiet is its flow;
And yet those hidden waters
    Have made the grass to grow!"

Then, "planted by the waters,"
    O Saviour, let me be,
That I may thus be fruitful,
    And glory bring to Thee!

Not unto me be glory!
Thy praises would I sing:
Yes, for the grass were nothing
Without the Secret Spring!

THE GOVERNMENT OF CHRIST.

Did this verse, "The government shall be upon *His* shoulder," ever speak peace to you concerning these things? Not merely the government of the universe, or of this world, or of the Church, but *His* government of *you*. No part of your life is a mistake or an accident, but every part of it is sent you straight from the Lord. Each day comes to you from Him; each circumstance, each event, each person you meet, each conversation you hold, each book that comes in your way, is ordered of Him. Every atom of your life comes to you from Him. The government of yourself is His daily ordering; it is your part to submit to that government; rather, to accept it, to go to Him morning by morning for orders for this one day. You know *He* will send you each circumstance, so ask Him to take it back *into His hands again.* Give Him yourself, but give Him also all the events of the day, confiding to His care those you know of, and begging Him to guard those you know not. Leave off governing yourself, and let Jesus do it.

Perhaps you say, "I don't know how to do this. A difficulty, a temptation comes, and before I have time to think, I am overcome." Perhaps it is a temptation that you know beforehand, will meet you. Then take it to Jesus, tell Him about it—*all* about it—and tell Him how it has overcome you, how quickly—how at the time you have been almost glad to yield, though it has been a grief afterward. Tell Him all about it, and that it is coming again, and then *leave* it with Him. Trust it and yourself to Him; do not worry, or fret, or fear. You have tried often to govern it yourself and have failed; do not try any more; let Jesus do it for you. Do you say: "I cannot. How can I expect Jesus to help me if I don't help myself?" What has all your helping yourself done for you? Nothing, but this one thing: it has *shown* you that all your efforts are vain. Now begin and trust to Jesus to do it for you. When the centurion whose servant was ill, came to Jesus, he simply stated his case. "My servant lieth at home sick of the palsy, grievously tormented." And Jesus said: "I will come and heal him." If the soldier had brought Jesus to his house, and then begun to try his own remedies, Jesus would have stood aside to let him prove how futile all his efforts were. Is He standing aside while you are busying yourself, hard at work, to cure your diseases? Dear soul, you are not the doctor; you are the patient. What a mistake you have been making all this time. Put it to rights quickly; give yourself entirely into the hands of Jesus—into His heart, I should rather say—and He will take you along with Himself, and cure you as you go, doing all *for* you.

WHAT JESUS SAYS TO ME.

FEAR not: for I have redeemed thee; I have called thee by thy name; thou art Mine. I, even I, am He that blotteth out thy transgressions, for mine own sake, and will not remember thy sins. Thou hast destroyed thyself, but in Me is thine help. Give *Me* thine heart; in vain shalt thou make thyself fair; from Me is thy fruit found. I will sprinkle clean water upon you, and you shall be clean; from all your filthiness and from all your idols, will I cleanse you. A new heart also will I give you, and a new spirit will I put within you; and I will take away the stony heart out of your flesh, and I will give you an heart of flesh, and I will put *My* spirit within you, and cause you to walk in My statutes, and you shall keep my judgments and do them. I will give you rest; My peace I give unto you. I also will keep thee from the hour of temptation. I will instruct thee and teach thee in the way which thou shalt go; I will guide thee with Mine eye. I am with thee, and will keep thee in all places whither thou goest. I will *never* leave thee nor forsake thee. My grace is sufficient for thee. If thou art not able to do that thing which is least, why take you thought for the rest? My strength is made perfect in weakness.

What wilt thou that I should do unto thee? Thou art careful and troubled about many things. Be careful for *nothing*, but come unto Me; I will help thee. Be not afraid; only believe. In quietness and confidence shall be your strength.

I have loved thee with an everlasting love, therefore with loving-kindness have I drawn thee. I know thee by name, and thou hast found grace in My sight. Now, therefore, if you will obey My voice indeed, and keep My covenant, you shall be a peculiar treasure unto Me. Behold thou art fair, My love, behold thou art fair; *perfect* through *My* comeliness put upon thee. Thou art *all* fair, My love; there is no spot in thee. I have blotted out as a thick cloud thy transgressions, and as a cloud thy sins. Why are you troubled, and why do thoughts arise in your heart? What will you that I shall do unto you? If you shall ask *anything* in My name, I will do it. Ask what you will, and it shall be done. Let not your heart be troubled, neither let it be afraid. Come near unto Me. As one whom his mother comforteth, so will I comfort you. Be of good cheer. These things have I spoken unto you that *My* joy might remain in you, and that your joy might be full.

MORE LIGHT NEEDED.

WHEN you are reading a book in a dark room, and come to a difficult part, you take it to a window to get more light. So take your Bibles to Christ.

A GOOD RULE FOR TRAVELLERS.

IT is a good and safe rule to sojourn in every place as if you meant to spend your life there, never omitting an opportunity of doing a kindness, or speaking a true word, or making a friend. Seeds thus sown by the wayside often bring forth an abundant harvest. You might so spend your summer among a people that they and their descendants should be better and happier, through time and eternity, for your works and your example.

NO CHOICE.

A CHRISTIAN lady, long confined to her bed by intense physical suffering, was asked what would be her desire could she know she might be fully restored to health? She replied, a sweet smile lighting up her countenance, "As the Lord will." "But if you are not to be restored?" suggested a friend. "Why, then it shall be as the Lord will," was her ready response. "But if you knew it to be His will, what would be your choice?" urged her friend. Closing her eyes, apparently committing all her interests to the dear keeping of infinite Love, she replied, "*Well then, truly, I should refer it to God.*"

MY SHEPHERD.

"He leadeth me!"
And so I need not seek my own wild way
    Across the desert wild;
He knoweth where the soft green pastures lie,
    Where the still waters glide,
And how to reach the coolness of their rest,
    Beneath the calm hill-side.

"He leadeth me!"
And though it be by rugged, weary ways,
    Where thorns spring sharp and sore,
No pathway can seem strange or desolate
    Where Jesus "goes before;"
His gentle shepherding my solace is,
    And gladness, yet in store.

"He leadeth me!"
I shall not take one needless step through all,
    In wind, or heat, or cold;
And all day long, He sees the peaceful end,
    Through trials manifold;
Up the fair hill-side, like some sweet surprise,
    Waiteth the quiet fold.

QUIETNESS IN SERVING.

No one can do more than He can, and the narrowest life is wider than most of our hearts. When people have a great many ways of doing good, they sometimes get so confused that they do nothing.

WORLDLY CONFORMITY.

Touching this subject, Adelaide Newton writes as follows to a schoolfellow:

"I cannot help thinking that if you are much occupied with thoughts of heaven, of holiness, of the meek and lowly Jesus, and how He lived and walked on earth, you will feel a secret shrinking from worldly society, which will make balls and such amusements very painful to you. God has left no positive commands upon things of this sort; for He knows that where the heart is given to Him, the life will assuredly be given too. And the motive of gospel-obedience is, not so much duty, as love. The child that loves its parents devotedly, or its friends, does what will please them at any cost. I hope," she adds, " you will not think me severe upon you in anything I have said; for you cannot think how I feel for you. My natural heart was so fond of the same worldliness, though in a different way. I struggled for months, or I may say, years, between God and the world; but never did I enjoy peace or happiness the whole time. No one knew what I endured. May you be spared the bitter conflict, and choose the better part at once and unreservedly."

> "Dead to the world, we dream no more
> Of earthly pleasures now;
> Our deep, divine, unfailing spring
> Of grace and glory—Thou!"

BE YE FOLLOWERS OF GOD.

THOU art to be in thy work a copyist, imitator of God. Now, whatever God does,

He does perfectly. If it be but the creation of a leaf or flower, it is done in such a manner as that the most minute and microscopic examination only serves to bring out fresh beauties. Strive to do thy work in such a manner. Let it be thy earnest effort that he who looks into it shall find no flaw. Let the thing not only be done, but be done gracefully and ornamentally, as far as may be. It is a great and precious thought that God may be pleased by service done with the whole soul, and with strict punctuality and conscientiousness.

CONSIDER ONE ANOTHER.

"The Lord turned the captivity of Job when Job prayed for his friends: also the Lord gave Job twice as much as he had before."

WHEN Job prayed for his friends the Lord turned his captivity. And I suppose it is generally by some simple means that

Doubting Castle is left behind; the sudden use of that key called Promise, or the mere effort to guide another soul out of the dark labyrinths of Giant Despair. For even in sorrow it is quite possible to think too much about one's self. As soon as Job looked at the wants of others he saw his own exceeding riches as a child of God; and presently Job had twice as much as he had before.

> Bury thy sorrow—
>   The world has its share—
> Bury it deeply,
>   Hide it with care.
> Think of it calmly
>   When curtained by night;
> Tell it to Jesus,
>   And all will be right."

A SOLEMN THOUGHT.

It is an old saying, and one of fearful and fathomless import, that we are here forming characters for eternity. Forming characters!

Whose? Our own, or others? Both; and in that momentous fact lies the peril and responsibility of our existence. Thousands of our fellow-beings will yearly, and till years shall end, enter eternity with characters different from those they would have carried thither had we never lived."

THE FATHERHOOD OF GOD.

When I consider how I feel toward my children, how I would clothe them with every inward excellence, and give them every outward opportunity; how my life is a kind of a school for them, to take them into a higher manhood—when I consider this, I think, "If I, being evil, know how to do this, what is the great soul of Jesus, which proves its love by dying for us? What must be the thought and desire of Christ for His household?" And if the little girl can come in from her frets and anxieties and sorrows, and hide her head in her mother's arms, and the mother will console her, and comfort her, and caress her, kissing away her tears, and send her out again, all brightened and happy, do you believe that the soul that nestles in the arms of Jesus Christ can go away without being comforted and consoled? Do not you believe that if you abide in Jesus Christ, He will do more for you than any earthly parent can do for a child? Every pain, and temptation, and burden, and care, and sorrow in life is to be alleviated by the grace of God, through the Lord Jesus Christ. There is provision for this very deliverance in the heart of the Saviour.

MY NEED AND THY LOVE.

A DEVOTED minister of Christ said on his dying bed that his religious experience was all expressed in these two verses:

> "O Saviour, I have naught to plead
> In earth beneath or heaven above,

>   But just my own exceeding need,
>   And Thy exceeding love.
>
> "The need will soon be past and gone—
>   Exceeding great but quickly o'er;
> The love unbought is all Thine own,
>   And lasts forevermore."

ONE OF THE JOYS OF HEAVEN.

WHEN I see dying Christians, they always seem to me, with their dim, closing eyes, like people who have gazed a long time at the sun, till, completely dazzled with its brilliance, their eyelids close. Oh! it must be delightful, out of the night of this earth and the dark death-chamber, to be received into the light of eternal life, and to complete and realize the text: "It doth not yet appear what we shall be." I have been thinking this Christmas-time, that when I get hence I will seek out one of the shepherds of Bethany, and get him to relate to me how they felt when they saw the glory of the

Lord hovering over them. Lately, as I was preaching about the deluge, and describing its terrors, I resolved to ask Noah to tell me the whole story. Indeed, I will begin at the beginning with Adam, and have the whole Bible history related to me gradually, and I am only afraid that eternity will be too short, especially when we come to the Passion, for then I shall get it related separately by every one who was present; and if St. Paul could say, even on earth, "I determined not to know anything amongst you save Jesus Christ and Him crucified;" or, "God forbid that I should glory save in the cross of our Lord Jesus Christ, by whom the world is crucified unto me, and I unto the world;" or when he tuned his song of triumph already upon earth: "Henceforth let no man trouble me; for I bear in my body the marks of the Lord Jesus"—what must it be to hear him in heaven glory in the Lord alone!

INWARD TRIALS.

ALL who desire conformity to Christ must be perfected with Him through manifold discipline. To some are appointed outward afflictions, to others spiritual difficulties. If rightly received, they are among God's richest blessings. But we are slow to recognize His hand in inward trials. We are depressed and cast down by the sight of our guilt and helplessness. We fear that our iniquity has come between us and God. We are in heaviness through manifold temptation. How apt is the poet's description of this dark experience!

> I asked the Lord that I might grow
>   In faith, and love, and every grace;
> Might more of His salvation know,
>   And seek more earnestly His face.
>
> 'Twas He who taught me thus to pray,
>   And He, I trust, has answered prayer;
> But it has been in such a way
>   As almost drove me to despair.

I hoped that in some favored hour,
    At once He'd answer my request;
And by His love's constraining power,
    Subdue my sins and give me rest.

Instead of this He made me feel
    The hidden evils of my heart;
And let the angry powers of hell
    Assault my soul in every part.

Yea, more, with His own hand He seemed
    Intent to aggravate my woe;
Crossed all the fair designs I schemed,
    Blasted my gourds, and laid me low.

"Lord, why is this?" I trembling cried,
    "Wilt Thou pursue Thy worm to death?"
"'Tis in this way," the Lord replied,
    "I answer prayer for grace and faith.

"These inward trials I employ,
    From self and pride to set thee free;
And break thy schemes of earthly joy,
    That thou mayest seek thy all in Me."

Secure, if possible, seclusion and quiet. The fear of interruption distracts the mind, and so does a feeling of haste.

Never begin to read without first lifting up to God an earnest request for His guidance, instruction, and blessing.

Study what Jesus says of the Holy Spirit (John xvi. 7, 13, 14, 15), until not a shadow of a doubt beclouds an habitual and affectionate remembrance of Him as your infallible teacher.

Do not attempt to read too much. Sometimes you will be able to read a chapter or several chapters with attention, facility, and profit; at other times, you will do better to pause upon a single verse. Analyze the verse; inquire how many thoughts does this verse contain; try if you can recall other verses which inculcate the same truth; inquire if the verse has any special application to yourself.

Read with your pen in hand, and note in your memorandum-book the thoughts which interest you. Study the Bible with unwearied endeavors to know and love Jesus, as you would study the letters of some friend whom you had never seen, but whom you wished to know and love.

Seek fresh thought. "Give us this day our daily bread" is the appropriate prayer of one who desires to feed upon the word of God. Yesterday's perceptions, impressions, and emotions will not suffice for to-day. They must be renewed and increased by to-day's study.

From each reading of the holy Scriptures, get at least one fresh, distinct, impressive thought, and dwell upon it. Many of the Psalms are prayers and praises. Select some one of these petitions or ascriptions of praise, adopt it as your own, and repeat it many times to God.

Sustain yourself by the remembrance that Bible-knowledge, like other knowledge, must increase from small beginnings. Unwearied patience and perseverance are indispensable; you must add thought to thought, prayer to prayer. Bible wisdom echoes the voice of God: "Ye shall seek me and find me, when ye shall search for me with all your heart."

Study the Bible with the utmost care to know yourself; to know the whole of your case, and especially to know wherein you fail to do the will of God.

THE SECRET OF SUCCESS.

IT is recorded of one of the Reformers, that when he had acquitted himself in a public disputation with great credit to his Master's cause, a friend begged to see the notes, which he had been observed to write, supposing that he had taken down the arguments of his opponents, and sketched the substance of his own reply. Greatly was he surprised to find that his notes consisted simply of the ejaculatory petitions—'More light, Lord—more light—more light!' And how fully was the true spirit of prayer compressed and illustrated in these short aspirations! Could they fail of success? "If any of you lack wisdom, let him ask of God, that giveth to all men liberally, and upbraideth not, and it *shall* be given him."

WHAT IS IT TO ABIDE IN JESUS?

To abide in Jesus is just to keep always the very attitude taken when Jesus was accepted.

As ye have received the Lord Jesus Christ, so walk ye in Him—rooted and grounded in Him, saith the apostle.

We received Him very humbly. We felt our place to be in the dust; our righteousness to be rags; our power to be weakness; and looked to Christ for all things.

Even so abide, so walk ye in Him. He who is lifted up with the idea of some exalted state of purity, or power, or safety gained, has in so far forgotten the apostolic injunction, and is not in the lowly way where Christ was received by him; his joy is in *his state,* not in Christ; his trust is in his own attainments, not in Christ.

The command is not—Now you have got into a high and holy state, so walk in *that,* but, Even as ye *received* Christ Jesus, so walk in Him.

MY DEBT TO CHRIST.

All that I *was*—my sin, my guilt,
My death was all my own;
All that I *am,* I owe to Thee,
My gracious God, alone.

The evil of my former state
  Was mine and only mine;
The good in which I now rejoice
  Is Thine and only Thine.

The darkness of my former state,
  The bondage all was mine;
The light of life in which I walk,
  The liberty is Thine.

Thy grace first made me feel my sin,
  It taught me to believe;
Then in believing, peace I found,
  And now I live, I live.

All that I am, e'en here on earth,
  All that I hope to be,
When Jesus comes and glory dawns,
  I owe it, Lord, to Thee.

FELLOWSHIP WITH JESUS.

BLESSED is he that understandeth what it is to love Jesus, and to despise himself for Jesus' sake.

When Jesus is present, all is well, and

nothing seems difficult; but when Jesus is not present, everything is hard.

Most poor is he who liveth without Jesus; and he most rich who is dear to Jesus.

Love Him, and keep Him for thy friend, who when all go away, will not forsake thee, nor suffer thee to perish in the end.

Amongst all, therefore, that be dear unto thee, let Jesus alone be especially beloved.

PILLOW PRAYERS.

He who knows nothing of pillow prayers is ignorant of one of the sweetest modes of prayer practicable on earth. The day with its engrossments being gone, it is a most favorable time for the gathering in of our thoughts upon ourselves—our sins, our wants, fears, and hopes, and then the turning of them up towards heaven. This is what the Psalmist is apparently referring to in his words, " When I remember thee upon my bed, and meditate upon thee in the night-watches." That he uttered many a pillow-prayer is a thousand-fold more than probable. "I have remembered thy name, O Lord, in the night." "I prevented the dawning of the morning and cried." Those cries were prayers before the dawn of day.

If these prayers of the pillow, however, be begotten only of sheer evening sloth, we may say of them that they are "bastards, and not sons." But if they are the legitimate children of weakness, excessive weariness, sickness, or other similar circumstances, then they are of the true house and lineage of heaven, coming down in kindredship all the way from Bethel, where the overjaded Jacob had his angelic vision on his pillow of stones.

Invalids, with your eyes so often held long waking in the night season, distrust not the pillow prayers. Hundreds are continually climbing to heaven by them, as on a ladder. If you, perchance, fall asleep in the act, do not fret about it. For what opiate from the shop of the apothecary is so harmless as such an out-breathing of your holiest desires upward? What is sweeter than to lose yourself in such a prayer? For prayer is simply a form of thought toward God, and nothing can be more fitting to the very last moments of daily consciousness than such thoughts.

"REST, WEARY SOUL!"

BE careful for *nothing*, in the calm and holy assurance that God is, for our sakes, caring for *everything*.

"OUR SINGLE ACRE."

FEW are needed to do the out-of-the-way tasks which startle the world, and one may be most useful just doing commonplace duties and leaving the issue with God. And when it is all over, and our feet will run no more, and our hands are helpless, and we have scarcely strength to murmur a last prayer, then we shall see that instead of needing a larger field, we have left untilled many corners of our single acre, and that none of it is fit for our Master's eye, were it not for the softening shadow of the cross.

TRUST HIM WHOLLY.

THE man who, after having cast his care on Christ, goes to fretting and worrying himself about anything or anybody, is like one who, having purchased a through ticket from here to—anywhere, and receiving a check for his baggage, gets out of the car at the end of a mile or two, and shouldering his trunk, starts to go the rest of the way alone. Christ never rolls back upon us burdens that we lay on Him; we take them back ourselves. What is a religion worth that will stay with a man in the sunshine, but clear out in a storm? The Christian has a right, and it is his duty, to be free from all care and anxiety. Let him lie on the promises, and be at rest. "Oh! but," says the doubting, worrying disciple, "the promises are made to the righteous; and I am so full of imperfections, I dare not claim them." Well, brother, if you wait for that righteousness which is by the law, you'll never be able to rest on the promises; but if you trust in Christ, *that* is counted to you for righteousness; and your right to the comfort of the promises is as good as though you were as holy as an angel. Christ's love sweeps away the unworthiness of all who sincerely love Him. God has undertaken for you; trust Him, though you know not where to get your next supply of bread.

A NOBLE LIFE.

Sir Thomas Fowell Buxton is said to have resembled, in his walk through the world, "a man passing through the wards of a hospital, and stooping down on all sides to administer help where it was needed."

DEPRESSION.

When we are uncomfortable and out of sorts—just sufficiently unwell not to be able to enjoy anything, but not incapacitated for exertion—it is a good rule at such a time to set ourselves resolutely to do something of which we shall be glad afterwards.

THE SECRET OF EDIFICATION.

To be true to God and to the thought of His presence all day long, and to let self occupy as little as possible of our thoughts; to care much for His approval, and comparatively little for the impression we are making upon others; to feed the inward light with oil, and then freely to allow it to shine—this is the great secret of edification.

HOME TRIALS.

"You know," I began, "dear Mrs. Campbell, that there are some trials that cannot do us any good. They only call out all there is in us that is unlovely and severe."

"I don't know of any such trials," she replied.

"Suppose you had to live with people who were perfectly uncongenial; who misunderstood you, and who were always getting into your way as stumbling-blocks?"

"If I were living with them and they made me unhappy, I would ask God to relieve me of this trial if He thought it best. If He did not think it best, I would then try to find out the reason. He might have two reasons. One would be the good they might do me. The other the good I might do them."

"But in the case I was supposing, neither party can be of the least use to the other."

"You forget, perhaps, the *indirect* good one may gain by living with uncongenial, tempting persons. First, such people do good by the very self-denial and self-control their mere presence demands. Then, their making one's home less home-like and perfect than it would be in their absence, may help to render our real home in heaven more attractive."

"But suppose one cannot exercise self-control, and is always flying out, and flaring up?" I objected.

"I should say that a *Christian* who was always doing that," she replied, gravely, "was in pressing need of just the trial God sent when He shut him up to such a life of hourly temptation. We only know ourselves and what we really are, when the force of circumstances brings us out."

"It is very mortifying and painful to find how weak one is."

"That is true. But our mortifications are some of God's best physicians, and do much toward healing our pride and self-conceit."

"Do you really think, then, that God *deliberately appoints* to some of His children, a lot where their worst passions are excited, with a desire to bring good out of this seeming evil! Why, I have always supposed the best thing that could happen to me, for instance, would be to have a home exactly to my mind; a home where all were forbearing and good-tempered; a sort of little heaven below."

"If you have not such a home, my dear, are you sure it is not partly your own fault?"

"Of course it is my own fault. Because I am very quick-tempered, I want to live with good-tempered people."

"That is very benevolent in you," she said, archly. I colored, but went on.

"Oh, I know I am selfish. And therefore I want to live with those who are not so. I want to live with those persons to whom I can look for an example, and who will constantly stimulate me to something higher."

"But if God chooses quite another lot for you, you may be sure that He sees you need something totally different from what you want. You said just now that you would gladly go through any trial in order to attain a personal love to Christ, that should become the ruling principle of your life. Now as soon as God sees this desire in you, is He not kind, is He not wise in appointing such trials as He knows will lead to this end?"

"MY PILGRIMAGE."

Trustingly, trustingly,
  Jesus to Thee
Come I ; Lord, lovingly
  Come Thou to me !
Then shall I lovingly
Then shall I joyfully
  Walk here with Thee.

Peacefully, peacefully
  Walk I with Thee ;
Jesus my Lord, Thou art
  All, all to me.
Peace Thou hast left us,
Thy peace hast given us ;
  So let it be.

Happily, happily,
  Pass I along,
Eager to work for Thee,
  Earnest and strong.
Life is for service true,
Life is for battle too,
  Life is for song.

THOUGHTS ON PUBLIC WORSHIP.

Do not allow public worship to degenerate into a mere saying of your private prayers in church. Think of the many others who are around you, of their sins, trials, wants, wishes, mercies—trying to throw yourself into their case. Be you praying and giving thanks for them, while they are praying and giving thanks for you. The closet is the place for laying down the *secret* burdens at the Throne of Grace. The church is the place for the intercommunion of saints with one another, and of all with God.

Be careful to make in an audible voice *all* the responses prescribed by the church. If persons around us in the congregation are merely silent auditors of the service, our own devotion is instantaneously chilled. If, on the other hand, they have all the appearance of earnest worshippers, devotion soon stirs and wakens up in our own heart. Throw, then, your contribution of heart, and soul, and sympathy into the service of the church, by making the responses simply and sincerely, in your natural voice.

THE LAW OF CHRIST.

It requires far more of the constraining love of Christ to love our cousins and neighbors as members of the heavenly family, than to feel the heart warm to our suffering brethren in Tuscany or Madeira. To love the whole Church is one thing; to love— that is, to delight in the graces and veil the defects of the person who misunderstood me and opposed my plans yesterday, whose peculiar infirmities grate on my most sensitive feelings, or whose natural faults are precisely those from which my natural character most revolts, is quite another.

But this need not be so. The daily intercourse of life might deepen our spiritual communion, instead of superseding it. Mutual infirmities, necessarily known to one another, and together confessed to the Father in heaven, may unite us more closely than common success and joy. If we could only learn, whilst dealing with our own infirmities as sins, to regard the faults of those dear to us, as we would regard their affections, being as tender and prayerful over their spiritual as we would over their bodily sickness; or, better still, if we could look on one another's faults as common enemies; blending with our every-day occupations and pleasures, the light of heavenly hopes and the energy of heavenly aims; praying together as those only can, the inmost secrets and homeliest details of whose lives are known to one another—our homes might indeed become sanctuaries, our families, the two or three gathered together in Christ's name, where He is in the midst; our social intercourse, as hallowed as our religious assemblies.

THE WAITING TIME.

No time of seeming inactivity is laid upon you by God without a just reason. It is God calling upon you to do His business by ripening in quiet all your powers for some higher sphere of activity which is about to be opened to you. The time is coming when you shall be called again to the front of the battle. Let that solemn thought of dread, yet kindling expectancy, fill the cup of your life with the inner work of self-development which will make you ready and prepared when your name is called. The eighteen years at Nazareth, what was their result? A few years of action, but of action concentrated, intense, infinite; not one word, not one deed, which did not tell, and which will not tell, upon the universe forever.

Eighteen years of silence, and then—the regeneration of the world accomplished, His Father's business done.

THE ETERNITY OF GOD.

Weak, weak, forever weak !
   We cannot hold what we possess ;
Youth cannot find, age will not seek—
   Oh, weakness is the heart's worst weariness :
But weakest hearts can lift their thoughts to Thee—
It makes us strong to think of Thine eternity !

Self-wearied, Lord, I come !
   For I have lived my life too fast ;
Now that years bring me nearer home,
   Grace must be slowly used to make it last ;
When my heart beats too quick, I think of Thee,
And of the leisure of Thy long eternity.

Then on Thy grandeur I wilt lay me down—
   Already life is heaven for me—
No cradled child more softly lies than I—
   Come soon, eternity !

WORLDLINESS.

HEART engrossment of any kind is worldliness to the Christian. Friendship, if it wholly absorb the heart, becomes worldliness. Duties, even those of religious benevolence, when proceeding from adulterated motives, or when monopolizing the mind so as to interfere with its ascent to the upper springs, fall into the low rank of things of the world.

A THOUGHT FOR FRIENDS.

"Love in life should strive to see
Sometimes what love in death would be."

SANCTITY in our friends and neighbors is like a star. We take no notice of the star while the sun is pouring his rays over the firmament, and the full stir of life is around us. But let the night draw her curtain over the sky; and the star in all its beauty steals out to view. So while our friends are mixed up with us in the hurry and commerce of life, we seem unable to disentangle from their infirmities the saintliness which is in them. But they die; and something comes to light about their inward life which hitherto had escaped every eye but God's, and we begin to discover that the commonest things they did were governed by Christian principle, and referred to God in prayer, and perhaps that we have been for years walking side by side with angels unawares. Death has now thrown his pall over them; they are no longer in the hubbub of life or the strife of tongues; and the star of their sanctity begins to twinkle brightly to our eyes. Oh! lest remorse, for having appreciated God's saints so little, should strike a chill to our hearts when they are taken from us, let us now be on the watch for any tokens of good in one another, and hail such tokens with affectionate reverence. Let not infirmities, however patent, blind our eyes to the grace which there may be in a brother. Let us hope for good in him, promptly believe in it, joyfully welcome it. And let us not fail to bless God for every example of faith and love given by His people, whether still in a state of warfare, or departed to their rest, beseeching Him to give us grace so to follow their good examples, that, with them, we may be partakers of His heavenly kingdom.

> How doth Death speak of our loved,
>   When it hath laid them low,
> When it hath set its hallowing touch
>   On lip and cheek and brow?
>
> It clothes their every gift and grace
> With radiance from the holiest place,
> With light as from an angel face.
>
> Recalling, with resistless force,
> And tracing to their hidden source,
> Deeds scarcely noticed in their course.

This little, loving, fond device,
That daily act of sacrifice,
Of which too late we learn the price.

Opening our weeping eyes to trace
Simple, unnoticed kindnesses,
Forgotten notes of tenderness.

Which evermore to us must be
Sacred as hymns in infancy,
Learned listening at a mother's knee.

Thus doth Death speak of our beloved,
  When it hath laid them low;
Then let Love antedate the work of death,
  And do this now!

MEDITATION.

It is not hasty reading, but seriously meditating upon holy and heavenly truths, that makes them prove sweet and profitable to the soul. It is not the bee's touching on the flowers, that gathers honey, but her abiding for a time upon them, and drawing out the sweet. It is not he that reads most, but he that meditates most on divine truth, that will prove the choicest, wisest, strongest Christian.

ENTER INTO THY CLOSET.

I FEEL all that I know and all that I teach, will do nothing for my soul if I spend my time, as some people do, in business or company. My soul starves to death in the best company, and God is often lost in prayers and ordinances. "Enter into thy closet," said He, and "shut thy door." Some words in Scripture are very emphatical. "Shut thy door" means much; it means, shut out, not only nonsense, but business; not only the company abroad, and the company at home; it means, let thy poor soul have a little rest and refreshment, and God have opportunity to speak to thee in a still, small voice, or He will speak to thee in thunder.

Come escape from the tempest of life,
   From the world to the desert retire ;
Quit this region of tumult and strife,
   To rekindle the heavenly fire.

Poor pilgrim ! thy strength must be sought
   In the heart-breathing accents of prayer ;
In public the battle be fought,
   But in secret the weapon prepare.

Oh, rest from thy labors awhile ;
   Go alone, on the mount, with thy Lord,
Go, bask in the beam of His smile,
   And feed on the wealth of His word.

ONENESS WITH CHRIST.

"LIFE is light." Live the truth, and the life of truth will shine from you. There is light evolved in all the developments of physical life on earth, were our senses fine enough to discern it. Life is the light of the world of spirit ; therefore spake Paul of " epistles written on the heart." Seize the distinction between an epistle written by a school-boy, painfully and formally, containing customary announcements, and the epistle of a friend, in which his heart freely discourses, and we meet with himself. You may find many a Christian, who, with pain and effort, writes something like the name of Christ on his life and actions, in which, however, the effort is palpable, the result formal or obscure. Christ sends us into the world that our frank and free communication may be full of Him; that when we most speak our hearts out, we may speak most of our Lord. His Father's mind was most manifest in Him when He most truly uttered His own mind; each deeper and truer manifestation, but manifested the unity more clearly; we see that at the very heart's core they were one. Is this your oneness? Have you to halt and check yourselves to watch and strive when you wish to do a Christ-like action, or manifest a Christ-like spirit; or does it flow from you like music from a heart full strung, or light from the fountain of day? I know it cometh not by course of nature—this heart-deep sympathy with Christ. I know it cometh but by strife and agony, through crucifying the desires of the flesh with more than human resolution, and by drinking the cup of the bitterness of sin to the very dregs; still it may come, it does come.

"If any man will come after me, let him deny himself, and take up his cross, and follow me." Explore the depth of that saying; have inwrought into the very texture of your spirit-life, the image of your Master, and then, whenever your nature is struck, it will sound like the Memnon's statue at the rosy flush of morning, and make the very air of this unholy world melodious with the name of its restored and rightful King.

LITTLE THINGS.

Christ comes to us morning by morning, to present to us, for the day then opening, divers little crosses, thwartings of our own will, interference with our plans, disappointments of our little pleasures. Do we kiss them, and take them up, and follow in His rear, like Simon the Cyrenian? Or do we toss them from us scornfully because they are so little, and wait for some great affliction to approve our patience and our resignation to His will? Ah, how might we accommodate to the small matters of religion generally, those words of the Lord respecting the children, "Take heed that ye despise not one of these little ones." Despise not little sins; they have ruined many a soul. Despise not little duties; they have been to many a saved man an excellent discipline of humility. Despise not little temptations; rightly met they have often nerved the character for some fiery trial. And despise not little crosses; for when taken up, and lovingly accepted at the Lord's hand, they have made men meet for a great crown, even the crown of righteousness and life, which the Lord hath promised to them that love Him.

THE KEEPING POWER OF CHRIST.

I REMEMBER a few years ago, in reading 2 Thess. ii., I came to the 13th verse, where Paul says, "We are bound to give thanks always to God for you, brethren, beloved of the Lord, because God hath from the beginning chosen you to salvation, through sanctification of the Spirit, and belief of the truth." "*Through sanctification of the Spirit.*" Here I paused, and read it over and over again; praying that God would sanctify me wholly by the Spirit. This verse comforted me many, many days. I felt that it was blessed to my soul, but the fulness of its meaning was not yet revealed to me. The inward currents of my heart were not stayed. I could not "*stand fast, therefore, in the liberty wherewith Christ hath made us free;*" for I was "entangled" again and "again with the yoke of bondage." I could not "reckon" myself "dead" to the perplexities and irritations of daily life, which a heart yearning for purity condemns as dishonoring to God. More earnestly than ever, and many times a day, I prayed for strength to overcome; but found no rest in my soul, until I stopped praying for *strength* to overcome, and *gave myself wholly to God to be kept*. At this time the Lord's Prayer became a new and wonderful revelation to me; I found, in its closing words, the full warrant for thus casting myself wholly on the Lord for deliverance. "And lead us not into temptation, but *deliver us from evil.* For thine is the *kingdom*, and the *power*, and the *glory*, forever, Amen." O how my soul was filled, as I realized for the first time that it was His *power* that was to keep me! "for Thine is the power."

The work was all done then; no more striving, no more praying for *strength* to overcome, but simply, day by day—

"Jesus, *keep* me, for Thine is the power and the glory;" and there *I rest and am kept.*

CASTING ALL ON JESUS.

I LEFT it all with Jesus
    Long ago ;
All my sin I brought Him,
    And my woe.
When by faith I saw Him
    On the tree,
Heard His still, small whisper,
    "'Tis for thee"—
From my heart the burden
    Rolled away—
    Happy day!

I leave it all with Jesus
    Day by day;
Faith can firmly trust Him,
    Come what may.
Hope has dropp'd her anchor—
    Found her rest,
In the calm, sure haven
    Of His breast;
Love esteems it heaven
    To abide
    At His side.

Oh! leave it all with Jesus,
    Drooping soul!
Tell not half thy story,
    But the whole.
Worlds on worlds are hanging
    On His hand.
Life and death are waiting
    His command;
Yet, His tender bosom
    Makes thee room—
    Oh, come home!

PRAYER A SERVICE.

We do not think enough what an effective service prayer is, especially intercessory prayer, direct application by name for others, laying their needs and cares, all they would or might request for themselves, before God. We do not believe as we should, how it might help those we so fain would serve, penetrating the hearts we cannot open, shielding those we cannot guard, teaching where we cannot speak, comforting where our words have no power to soothe; following the steps of our beloved through the toils and perplexities of the day, lifting off their burdens with an unseen hand at night. No ministry is so like that of an angel's as this—silent, invisible, known but to God; through us descends the blessing, and to Him alone ascends the thanksgiving. Surely not an employment brings us so near to God and the spirits of men, as intercessory prayer. There is a depth of wisdom in the words, "If we only spoke more to God for man, than even to man for God!"

MENTAL GROWTH.

I WOULD have every man of close occupation, make it a sacred duty to keep up a living knowledge of, and interest in, some pursuit, science, art or craft, outside the circle of his daily task. Thereby he will keep his mental faculties in fair play upon their appointed objects, and lay up for himself a pursuit and an education, which will occupy nobly and happily the autumn of life. What men want, is something to carry on their education till they die, something which will continually draw them out to fresh observation, fresh reflection, fresh acquisition, with ever stronger and riper power. Clip a bit from your daily earnings, rather than from your daily study. The play, and even the strain of the faculties—the various faculties of body, and mind, and spirit, in wise proportions and alternations—is the true human joy. Plenty to think of, plenty to observe, plenty to pursue, plenty to delight in, plenty to help, plenty to love, these make the gladness and the riches of the being.

SILENT LIVES.

How many there are, and how useful. Think of the monotonous, unknown, unpretending work of the mother of a family. What a sameness of life, what a continual routine of voiceless, seemingly insignificant duties! Little tender services, little watchful services, little watchful teachings, little grave checkings, little gentle guidings—line upon line—here a little and there a little. Little anxious yearnings, little quiet prayers—and so the life goes on, and if her heart be longing to spend and be spent in her dear Lord's service, perhaps she has her dull hours of depression; she is doing nothing, can do nothing, she fears, for Christ. Nothing? O silent lives! how much, how very much you may do in this world, where so much has to be done! Mere gentleness and kindliness, taught by God's Spirit—of this we can hardly overvalue the influence and effect. But to have a nest of Christ's little ones to rear for Him, and this with the certainty of His aid in answer to prayer—what shall we say of this? O work! to undertake which, the sweetest-toned harp in heaven might be gladly laid down!

> "It may be thy share of service
>   His purpose to complete,
> If steadfastly thou guidest
>   Those little wayward feet.
>
> "One little footstep passing
>   The path that Jesus trod;

> One little spirit resting
> In loving faith on God;
>
> "One little life more earnest,
> More hopeful, and more pure—
> And in an angel's record
> Thy life-work shall endure."

OUR WORK HELD IN EVERLASTING REMEMBRANCE.

No good that the humblest of us has wrought ever dies. You are a teacher. If you have been faithful, some good has flowed from you into the mind and heart of your pupil, and, perhaps, he was aware of it at the time. But by and by, other influences lend their aid to form his mind and character, and what you have done cannot be distinguished from newer forces, which act on the youth and on the man. Perhaps you have thrown some seed into his mind, which after long years bears fruit, and he ascribes the good to some one else. What then? If you have served God in serving him, God remembers it, although he does not. There is one, long, unerring memory in the universe, out of which nothing good ever fades.

ABIDING IN CHRIST.

It is not so much working for God, or speaking for God, as living in the secret of His presence which most glorifies Him. We must so seek to realize our Saviour's presence with us, and in us, that our whole being should be hushed, and quietly elevated, and controlled in every little thing, and little word; thus we shall glorify Him, and shall become a power in His hands among men.

GOD'S WAYS OF ANSWERING PRAYER.

At a meeting of a few Christian people, which I attended in a foreign city, a clergyman, speaking of prayer, said: "God sometimes answers at once; sometimes He gives us some better thing in the place of the particular thing we ask; sometimes he answers by the very contrary of what we wished, and out of that, springs the particular thing that we prayed for."

SPIRITUAL WEAKNESS.

Be assured that one cause of spiritual weakness is the constant dwelling upon self instead of upon Christ. Such persons study self more than they study Christ, and then they are weak in courage—they have none; weak in power—they can do nothing; weak in love—it centres all in itself. There is no expansiveness; there is no going forth to others. Why, how constantly we see it, my brethren—persons that are in affliction, perhaps unable to get out much, to have much intercourse with others. A great many persons visit them, but it is always in the way of sympathy, giving out to them, compassionating them, pitying them, making them think still more and more of self. But when those persons recover a little, let them make an effort, and go to see other people, and give out to others, instead of always craving to take in, and how wonderfully they are improved. What a change it makes when once we are occupied with the sorrows of others instead of always circling just round our own.

Oh, it is not good for some minds always to be taking in human sympathy, but it is a good thing to be giving out. The happiest are those that have large sympathies for the sorrows of others; who endeavor to cast their own cares upon the Lord, and who receive from Him that help and support by which they are comforted themselves, and enabled to comfort others. As I have said, then, these persons are weak because they look in, and not out—down, and not up; so they forget what Christ is, and dwell only on what they themselves are—poor and wretched and miserable. They forget all the promises of God, and that His Word is like Himself—'The same yesterday, to-day, and forever.'

ONE LIFE.

'Tis not for man to trifle! Life is brief,
    And sin is here.
Our age is but the falling of a leaf,
    A dropping tear.
We have no time to sport away the hours,
All must be earnest in a world like ours.

Not many lives, but only one have we,
    One, only one!
How sacred should that one life ever be,
    That narrow span!
Day after day filled up with blessed toil,
Hour after hour still bringing in new spoil.

THE PRECIOUS BLOOD.

It is precious to the believer, for it is his staff and his stay in all his pilgrimage. He goes daily to the fountain opened for sin and all uncleanness, for it has been the lesson of his Christian life to know his weakness and corruptions, and the necessity of a ransom greater than he can pay.

As the Holy Spirit has uncovered to his vision the deep depravity of his heart, as his besetting sins have often carried him to the verge of despair, as he sees himself and knows himself so differently from what the world sees and believes him to be, as days of sickness and loss come with their doubts and fears and sorrows, as the "dark valley" looms up, (though it may be a long way off,) even with more darkness and dread than when near at hand, "the precious blood" is unspeakably precious; for it is his only reliance, his only hope. Nothing else will comfort, nothing else will strengthen, nothing else will save.

The blood of Jesus, shed on the cross for his sins, past, present and to come, the full, sufficient, complete payment forever, not because he is good or that he first loved God, but because God first loved him and gave Himself a sacrifice and propitiation for his sins.

There are believers who will never enter into the fulness of joy that this truth should give them, until they shall see Him as He is. They can understand why the sick go to the physician all the days of their sickness. They love the man who has delivered from debt and imprisonment, his neighbor who could not pay his creditor, and can fully realize that the obligation to that creditor has been fully discharged forever; but their sins and repeated falls accuse them and make them doubt even to the last.

But they never turn away from their faith in "the precious blood," but cling to it as their only hope and trust, and through it they will be abundantly saved and their doubts and self-condemnation shall be buried in the ocean of His righteousness, and their joy shall be full.

"The precious blood" has given us all that is good and blessed here. It lightens all our sorrows and sweetens all our joys. As it purchased for us eternal life, so has it brought us our earthly comforts and given us strength for each day's trials and troubles. It gives contentment in the home of the poor, resignation and peace in the house of mourning, patience and submission in the chamber of sickness. The aching heart looks to it as its only refuge, the thankful and cheerful know that its blessed gifts are the source of all their earthly good. The departing soul more than ever knows that "the precious blood" has washed away every stain, and prepared for it an inheritance incorruptible, undefiled, and that fadeth not away.

The precious blood of Christ, the beginning and the end, the source of all true joy on earth, the only ransom that will be accepted in heaven, what shall we offer in its stead in that day when God shall judge the world?

PAST TROUBLES.

How many troubles, my friends, you have been through! And the Lord has sustained you in every one. Where are the troubles of last year? Look back at them. How many were there? You cannot count them. You have only a vague idea of them. You may have passed through bankruptcy, or there may have been a death in your family; but aside from these, you have no distinct recollection of the troubles that you have had within the past year. That brood of things which lowered the whole tone, the temperature of your spirituality, and made those wrinkles on your brow—what became of them? Did they hinder you or hurt you?

THE VOICE OF THE BLOOD.

"The blood of Jesus pleads."—Reid.

O BLOOD of Jesus, plead for me!
 Attend my fainting cry;
Take Thou the word I cannot say,
Within the holy place to-day,
 While in the dust I lie.

O blood of Jesus, plead for me!
 Say, "I the debt have paid;"
Say, "I the law have quite fulfilled,
Now must its fierce demands be stilled,
 No charge to her is laid."

O blood of Jesus, plead for me!
 Plead for the blind and weak,

Say, "I her surety still will be;
E'en though her help she fail to see,
  I her sad cause will speak."

O blood of Jesus, plead for me!
  Behold my awful need!
Say, "Here my power I must display,
Sin's deepest dye to wash away—
  A power to cleanse indeed."

O blood of Jesus, plead, still plead!
  A holy God I flee;
Say, "*I* her case will undertake—
Her *desperate* case, and sweetly make
  Peace, 'twixt this soul and Thee."

TRUE REST.

THE active mind, if out of its proper sphere, corrodes itself, and frets itself with plans and projects, finding no rest. The rest of Christ is not that of torpor, but harmony; it is not refusing the struggle, but conquering *in it;* not resting *from* duty, but finding rest *in* duty.

ON HELPING THE POOR.

GIVING is the smallest and easiest part of Christian charity. Time is far more precious, and effort is far more precious than money to hard-worked men. And money may be given lavishly to save time and trouble, and may very easily be, nay, it too constantly is, a curse instead of a blessing to the poor. The Lord had no money to give, nor would He make any. This last is among the most significant features of His ministry. And the poorest Christian ministers are probably those who at this moment are doing the most for the help of the poor.

The poor are commonly their own worst enemies. Their own improvidence, carelessness, and vice share fully with the condition of society, the responsibility of their state. They are very far from being their true friends who are afraid to tell them so—who will throw a sop of charity to meet their momentary need and to win their passing gratitude, instead of tenderly but firmly pressing on them the recognition of the evil habits and passions, out of which, after all, nine-tenths of their evil spring. To cure an evil habit, to brighten a sullen temper, to conquer a vicious propensity in the poor subjects of your ministry, is to give something which is infinitely more precious than gold; it is a gift which they may bear on with them into eternity.

THE EXAMPLE OF OUR MASTER.

How much even of our graces is offered to man rather than to God! Even in our most devoted service, what a seeking there is, perhaps unconsciously, to be something in the estimation of others; some secret desire, some undetected wish, even by our very service to be greater here! The very gifts of God and the power of His Spirit are sought, the better to give us a place in this world. Thus are our very graces used to obtain for us glory, not of God, but of those around us. Surely this is one of the reasons why God can trust us with so little, for with His gifts we build up our own name, instead of His name.

But how unlike all this is to our Master; yea, how unlike even to His Apostles! "Neither of men," says Paul, "sought we glory, neither of you, nor yet of others." This is our calling, not only to be nothing in the world, but to be willing to be nothing even among our brethren; to take the nearest place to Him, who has indeed taken the lowest.

Christ's example is one most precious to us. His service to His neighbor was always "*an offering unto the Lord.*" Thus He gladly was spent for others, though the more He loved them, the less He was loved.

May we be thus like Him, that so through grace we may be steadfast. If, on the other hand, our labor of love is offered for man's acceptance, when man rejects us, our labor will cease. And surely this is the secret of much of our half-hearted service. But let us, when ministering to others, offer ourselves, like Jesus, "unto the Lord," and not unto man; then, though our love is here slighted, it will be accepted by Him to to whom we offer it.

HE KNOWETH OUR FRAME.

He knoweth our frame: He remembereth that we are dust.—Ps. ciii. 14.

Lord, is it wrong—this state of things?
   I hardly know :
Each little bird its anthem sings ;
   I feel so low,
So restless, so disheartened, and so weary !
Life seems to me so desolate and dreary !

This body seems to drag me down :
> I cannot see

The beautiful, unfading crown,
> Prepared for me.

Some of Thy children seem so full of light !
But as for me, my day is almost night !

I do believe it was for me
> That Jesus died :

And Heaven's door, I think I see,
> Is opened wide :

I do believe that He will let me in,
And that His blood has cleansed me from my sin.

Oh ! why then should I feel afraid ?
> Is it not true,

My sins were all on Jesus laid,
> And sorrows too ?

Hath He not grace enough for all to-morrows ?
For surely He hath borne our griefs and sorrows !

My Father ! O how sweet the name !
> Art Thou not near ?

Say, dost Thou pity me ? or blame ?
> I long to hear !

Father ? My Father ! This is all my trust,
That Thou rememberest I am but dust !

Thou knowest well my frame, for Thou
          Hast fashioned me:
The darkness all around me now
          Is light, to Thee!
Then take me by the hand, and lead me on,
Thy poor blind child, until the night be gone!

Until the shadows flee away
          Before the sun,
And glorious, everlasting Day
          Shall have begun!
Meanwhile, in love and pity, lead Thou me.
For all my expectation is from Thee!

THE SPIRIT'S GUIDING.

As a man increases in earnest love to Christ, a delicate tact grows up within him, a spiritual instinct, which teaches him what he ought to say and do, and what he had better avoid on each particular occasion. True love, even human and earthly love, is full of sensibilities; every one is aware how a person, whom he loves and seeks to please, will take a thing; without being wrong or coarsely offensive, it would be simply out of taste to say or do such and such things before such a person; they would jar upon him. There is something of the same kind in divine love, the true lover of Christ being made sensitive by the Holy Spirit as to the line of conduct which pleases or displeases Him. "I will instruct thee and teach thee in the way which thou shalt go;" this is God's gracious promise by the Psalmist; and "*I will guide thee with mine eye.*" "Be ye not as the horse, or as the mule, which have no understanding; whose mouth must be held in with bit and bridle." Everybody knows what the guidance of a mother's eye is, while the children are around her. She need not speak. A glance and the expression of her countenance convey her wishes sufficiently. She looks up in alarm, and her eye warns the little ones away from danger;

they are industrious, and her eye betokens approval; or they are too frolicsome, and a look of displeasure checks them. God's children, too, know the meaning of His eye. They know, by the glance He gives them, what path He would have them pursue, and what avoid. He never leaves them without an interior indication of His will, if they have but one desire, that of pleasing Him.

HIS ANSWER.

A CHRISTIAN friend, calling upon a poor old woman in Scotland, found her in great pain, and expressed sorrow at seeing her suffer so much. "Oh," said Jeannie, "it's just an answer to prayer. You see, I've lang prayed to be conformed to the image of Christ. And since this is the means, I've naething to do wi' the choosin' o' them. It is ours to aim at meetness for His presence, and to leave it to His wisdom to take His ain way wi' us. I would rather suffer than sin, ony day."

LOVE THE FULFILLING OF THE LAW.

A MAN may have very strong conscientiousness; he may be a just man, and a true man, and a moral man, and yet not have the critical test of Christianity; for that test is love. A man may have great fervor in prayer; he may have great fervor in all forms of social devotion; he may be rapturous and exceedingly happy; and yet he may not have a critical test of Christianity. It is not fervor. It is not devoutness, though it includes devoutness. It is benevolence. It is the power to love. He who knows how to throw out a flame from his affections; he who knows how to make persons around him, wherever he goes, happy; he who knows how to do it morning, and noon, and night; he who knows how to make love his uniform disposition; he who knows how to radiate sympathy, and gentleness, and kindness, and forbearance, and patience toward others, and to make men feel richer for his being with them—he has the critical test of piety. It is to do by men what the sunshine does by you—make them cheerful, and full of life, and full of love, and full of fruit. These are the New Testament tests of Christian character.

NOT LOST.

The look of sympathy, the gentle word,
Spoken so low that only angels heard;
The secret art of pure self-sacrifice,
Unseen by men, but marked by angels' eyes;
  These are not lost.

The sacred music of a tender strain,
Wrung from a poet's heart by grief and pain,

And chanted timidly, with doubt and fear,
To busy crowds who scarcely pause to hear ;
   It is not lost.

The silent tears that fall at dead of night,
Over soiled robes which once were pure and white ;
The prayers that rise like incense from the soul,
Longing for Christ to make it clean and whole ;
   These are not lost.

The happy dreams that gladdened all our youth,
When dreams had less of self and more of truth ;
The childlike faith, so tranquil and so sweet,
Which sat like Mary at the Master's feet ;
   These are not lost.

The kindly plans devised for others' good,
So seldom guessed, so little understood ;
The quiet, steadfast love that strove to win
Some wanderer from the woeful ways of sin ;
   These are not lost.

Not lost, O Lord, for in that city bright
Our eyes shall see the past by clearer light ;
And things long hidden from our gaze below,
Thou wilt reveal, and we shall surely know
   They were not lost.

THE ART OF BEING MISERABLE.

KINGSLEY says: "If you should wish to be miserable you must think about yourself; about what you want, what you like, what respect people ought to pay to you, what people think of you; and then to you nothing will be pure. You will spoil everything you touch; you will make sin and misery for yourself out of everything which God sends you; you will be as wretched as you choose."

HOW TO WORK.

LET it be firmly settled in the mind before we put our hand to the work, and let us suffer the mind from time to time to revert to the thought that what we are about to do is the task assigned to us in the order of God's providence; that it is a task which He will inspect, and that it must be executed as well as ever we are able, in order that it may meet His approval. There are children who are too young to be left alone in the preparation of their lessons. The teacher must sit with them while they prepare; they must work under his eye, and have him by them to apply to, and ask help from him, when they come across a difficulty. Now some of the deepest lessons of divine truth are to be learned from our management of children; and the way of so doing work, as that it may be a source of spiritual consolation and strength, is among these lessons. Do the work under the eye of your heavenly Master; and look up in His face from time to time, for His help and blessing; an internal colloquy with Him, ever and anon, so far from being a distraction, will be a furtherance. For no work can in any sense prosper which is not done with a bright, elastic spirit, and there is no means of keeping the spirit bright and elastic but by keeping it near to God. Do but keep as close under His eye when working as you can contrive to do, and open your heart to Him as often as you can.

THE THING THAT I LONG FOR.

Thou, O Lord God, art the thing that I long for.—Ps. lxxi. 4. (Prayer-Book Version.)

> Thou art the thing that I long for,
> Though there are beautiful things,
> Things to delight and enrapture,
> Even in earth's "nether springs."
>
> Thou art the thing that I long for!
> Give Thyself wholly to me!
> Other things crumble and vanish;
> Nothing contents me but Thee!
>
> Thou art the thing that I long for!
> Lord, I believe Thou art near!
> Where could these longings find utterance,
> But in Thy listening ear?
>
> Thou art the thing that I long for!
> Yes, and this longing of mine,

Though almost dumb from intenseness,
Is but the echo of Thine!

Thou art the thing that I long for!
O that each sorrow I feel,
O that each loss and bereavement
More of Thyself may reveal!

Thou art the thing that I long for!
Heaven itself will be fair,
Fair in its glorious completeness,
Chiefly because Thou art there!

A CLOSER WALK.

"KEEP close intimacies with Jesus," wrote one who had proved the blessedness of a Divine companionship. "Oh! believe that God is near you at all times. Cultivate a close acquaintance. Let Him not be out of sight. If we walk at a distance from a friend, and see him but seldom, our knowledge of him is but limited; but if we live with him, dwell in the same habitation, we learn his character. Oh! let an aged Christian urge on your mind a closer walk with God. Be much in communion with Him."

In these days of Christian activity, how needful are these holy admonitions! Work for Christ too often absorbs the mind and leaves it with little time or inclination for communion with Him. Heavenly-mindedness may be preserved amidst the seen and temporal, but it is born of the unseen and eternal. It must be cherished by daily communion with God. Alone with Him, the soul is fed, strengthened, and refreshed. It is prepared for life. A close abiding fellowship with Christ! Who that has tasted its preciousness would relinquish it for all the pleasures of earth? An ever-increasing acquaintance with Christ should be the aim of every believer. He is ready —ready for the closest friendship that can be realized here—ready to lead the willing soul to the perfect fellowship of the redeemed in heaven.

ON RELIGIOUS CONVERSATION.

Let me give, in one word, the remedy of all the falseness, shallowness, and emptiness of religious conversation; the key to those stores of reality, earnestness, and naturalness, which will attract rather than disgust, where there is any good ground yet to be got at under the growing surface of rock which the world forms upon the heart. The secret is unmasked to us by the Great Teacher.

"Out of the abundance of the heart the mouth speaketh."

Thus we have the recipe. If we would talk continually, easily, naturally of course, and with a ready finding (not making) of opportunities, here we are taught the method. Let our heart be full of the love of God, full of devotion to our dear Saviour, and of kindly yearning for those about us: let such abundant stores be accumulated in the heart, and surely there must from time to time be produced some samples on the tongue. Let the great end of life and its mighty realities be indeed and, as a rule, the first things in our heart; and then they will hardly be always the last things on the lips. Let us be setting our life daily to the pattern of Christ's life, and assuredly then something of that ever-ready and unforced speaking of Christ concerning His Father's business—not dragged into but flowing from the ordinary talk—indeed, suggested by it, and growing out of it—some dim reflections of this ideal of religious conversation, of all conversation, would be traceable in our intercourse with friends certainly, and even with ordinary acquaintances.

Thus on Sundays, it should not be, if our hearts were in the day, a restraint to talk, but *relief* to talk out of the *abundance* of the heart, of the things of Christ and of God. Truly it does seem hardly natural that we, waiting upon the shore for the boat to take us off, should preserve ever a discreet silence concerning all but the pebbles and the shells under our feet.

The abundance of the heart—that will influence the talk; and you can't make the sham at all like the real thing. The abundance of the tongue merely will disgust. I do not think the *heart's* wealth would ever do this. It might, indeed, rather sadden where the hearer perceived, but could not appreciate its reality.

THE DAY A MINIATURE LIFE.

THE day is a life in little, a miniature life. Let a convex mirror be suspended overhead in a room, so as to form a small angle with the wall; you will see all the whole room in it, wide as it may be, with all the details of the furniture, and all the company. And how is this? Every object is, of course, greatly reduced in size, so that every square yard of space in the room appears as a square inch of space, or less, on the mirror. Still there is nothing which finds its place in the room which does not also find a proportionate place on the mirror. So it is with the day and the life-time. The day is the convex mirror of life. Do you desire a summary estimate of a man's whole character, as it will appear upon a calm review after he is laid in his coffin? Study him for a day only, from his rising to his lying down; and it is enough; the germs of the life are in the day; and that microscopic view, aided by a little effort of imagination, puts you in possession of the whole truth respecting him. Is it not written, "He that is faithful in that which is least, is faithful also in much"; and he that is unjust in the least, is unjust also in much"?

ANOTHER DAY.

Another page of life
  Is opened unto me;
O blessed Spirit! write thereon
  What seemeth best to Thee.

Write lovely acts of love;
  Write holy thoughts of praise;
Yea, write a copy, Spirit dear,
  Of one of Jesus' days.

And every mark of mine—
  Oh! wash it, wash it white;
Let nothing on the page appear,
  But words that Thou dost write.

And then, lest some should miss
Whence all the goodness came,
When Thou hast written all the rest,
Write underneath Thy name.

"HOW TO ENTER INTO REST."

Perhaps it is years since Jesus stood and knocked at the door, and you heard His voice, and opened the door, and He came in, and sat down to sup with you. And yet all this time it has hardly seemed as if He were inside; for you say it has been so different to what you hoped—you are so little changed, so little different. Perhaps this may be the reason; you let Him in, and He sat down to sup with you, and you found it wonderfully sweet to have Him. But you have treated Him as a Visitor; you have still arranged your own house, swept it yourself, garnished it yourself, cleansed it yourself, repaired it yourself. Some day you expect to go to His own house. That will be a very lovely place, you think, and you long to be going there. Your own house is so small; you have such work to keep it in anything like order; it tires you so and worries you, and you have hardly time to think of your Visitor, you are so busy making the place fit for Him. Oh! poor, loving, weary soul, He did not come to be a Visitor; He came to be the *Master* of your house. Throw all the doors open to Him; tell him you can do nothing with it; put yourself at His feet, and ask Him to take it all, just as it is, and He will rise and gird Himself, and come forth and serve you. Your house shall become His home, and He will make it bright and lovely by his presence. Then He will teach you to serve. Together you will work, and how you will learn to trust and love the Master-workman!

He may cast many things aside as useless. You will grieve to see them go; but you will know you cannot have both them and Him. He will not send you to work alone; He will always be with you. He will not tire you, nor let you tire yourself. He will not work you too quickly, but graciously and gently, and His presence, His part, His share in it all will be your rest.

Then put your whole trust in Him, and He will be with you—

<blockquote>"To cleanse and keep you clean."</blockquote>

WAIT ON THE LORD.

There are two bitter enemies of man's true life—the world without him, and the world within him—the world in his heart. The conflict is sometimes terrible, and thou dost sometimes feel as one left without strength, and thy hands fail, and thy heart grows faint. What is this but to teach thee where thy true strength lies, and to cast thee off from every other? "Wait on the Lord; be of good courage; and He shall strengthen thy heart. Wait, I say, on the Lord."

Sometimes the discouragement is deeper yet. We live under the hidings of our Master's face. He seems to have covered Himself with a thick cloud, which our sight cannot pierce, and which our prayers cannot pass through—they fall consciously short of their aim, and come back to the dull earth, flat and unprofitable. But be of good cheer. This cannot last forever nor last long. Only "rest in the Lord, and wait patiently for Him;" and be assured that "the Lord is good to them that wait for Him;" and although it may be that now, for a little while, thou liest void of strength, and almost lifeless upon the ground, yet, amid this chilliness, still wait;

though wounded, wait — holding fast the conviction which His promise gives. "They that wait upon the Lord shall renew their strength. They shall mount up with wings as eagles; they shall run and not be weary; they shall walk and not faint."

FAR OFF, YET NEAR.

O BLESSED Lord!
Once more, as at the opening of the day,
    I read Thy Word;
And now, in all I read, I hear Thee say,
"To those who love I will be ever near;"
    And yet while this I hear,
To me, O Lord, Thou seemest far away.

Thou Sovereign One,
Greater than mightiest kings, can it be fear,
    Or blinding sun
Made by Thy glory, so if Thou art here,
  I cannot see Thee; yet this word declares
    That whoso loves and bears
Thy Holy Name shall have Thee ever near!

FOR DAILY LIFE.

      I bear Thy name :
That love, dear Lord, have I not long confessed?
      Thy love's the same
As when, like John, I leaned upon Thy breast,
  And knew I loved : oh ! which of us has changed?
  Am I from Thee estranged ?
O Lord, Thou changest not ; I know the rest.

      My doubting heart
Trembles with its own weakness, and afraid,
      I dwell apart
From Thee, on whom alone my hope is stayed ;
  I would, and yet I do not know Thy will
  And perfect love—and still
Trusting myself, to be by self betrayed.

      O blessed Lord !
Far off, yet near, on me new grace bestow,
      As in Thy Word
I go to meet Thee ; even now, I know
  Thou nearer art than when my quest began ;
  One cry, and Thy feet ran
To meet me ; Lord, I will not let Thee go !

BE SATISFIED WITH CHRIST.

Not a few are more anxious to have the gifts of the Holy Spirit than the Spirit Himself, as an indwelling One, desiring the *gift* rather than the *giver;* longing for what Jesus gives, rather than Jesus Himself. How would you feel had you given to a friend a precious jewel as a token of love, expecting it to be a living remembrancer of yourself, and, lo and behold! you soon discover that your gift was so highly prized, so absorbing all the thoughts, as to leave no place in the heart for yourself, and hence you had been forgotten? Let me counsel you to seek for nothing beyond Christ. Let your thoughts centre in Him. Be satisfied with Christ. Having chosen you for His bride, and made you "comely in his comeliness," resign yourself to his love. Rest in His embrace; trusting on the fulfilment of His promise: "My grace is sufficient for you." And be assured the needed power for the service He assigns you will not be withheld. Remember it is *His* service in which you are to engage—not yours—so you may well leave the issue of it all to Him. The advancement of His own glory in the service, will secure to you an endowment of power in measure equal to the emergency, and as often as occasions for its exercise shall occur.

ON HABIT.

To establish a habit, we have only to continue doing the act which is to constitute it. The nature of the habits we form determine our character.

Every action we perform, every thought that crosses the mind, every emotion we feel, is in reality the beginning of a habit. If the habit be never established, it will be only because the state of mind indicated by the action, the thought, the emotion, has not been repeated sufficiently often to awaken and determine upon it the strength of the iterative power. When once this power is worked up to its full force, and directed in any line of thought, emotion, or action, it will carry the mind along that line with a force it has no power to resist. It may be compared to a mountain torrent. When it first breaks forth, it wanders for a time uncertainly, but having once worn for itself a channel, it will settle down to it, and continue in it forever.

THE DANGER OF NEGLECTING PRAYER.

ONE word about prayer. It is a preparation for danger, it is the armor for battle. Go not, my Christian brethren, into the dangerous world without it. You kneel down at night to pray, and drowsiness weighs down your eyelids. A hard day's work is a kind of excuse, and you shorten your prayer, and resign yourself softly to repose. The morning breaks, and it may be you rise late, and so your early devotions are not done, or done with irregular haste. No watching unto prayer; watchfulness once more omitted. And now we ask is that reparable? Brethren, we solemnly believe not. There has been that done which cannot be undone. You have given up your prayer, and you will suffer for it. Temptation is before you, and you are not fit to meet it. There is a guilty feeling on the soul, and you linger at a distance from Christ. It is no marvel if that day in which you suffered drowsiness to interfere with prayer, be a day on which you betrayed Him by cowardice and soft shrinking from duty. Let it be a principle through life; moments of prayer intruded upon by sloth cannot be made up. We may get experience, but we cannot get back the freshness and strength which were wrapped up in these moments.

"JESUS ONLY."

Dear Lord, only Thee, only Thee, I pray,
  Fill my heart with only Thee,
Till I shall pass away.
  Many do I love, and many do love me,
But Thou, Thou all above,
  Thou knowest I love Thee.

Dear God, be my guide,
I give my hand to Thee;
By day and night,
  Through time and tide,
I know Thou wilt keep me.
  The fairest love is mine
Which in this world may be.
  Dear Lord, let ever Thine be mine,
Thou knowest I love Thee.

WHAT HE IS ABLE TO DO.

Able even to subdue all things unto Himself.

Able to make all grace abound toward you: that you, always having all-sufficiency in all things, may abound to every good work.

Able to keep you from falling, and to present you faultless before the presence of His glory with exceeding joy.

Able to succor them that are tempted.

Able also to save them to the uttermost that come unto God by Him.

What He had promised, able also to perform.

Able to make us stand.

Able to keep that which I have committed to Him:

Able to build you up, and to give you an inheritance among all them that are sanctified.

Able to do exceedingly abundant above all that we ask or think.

Believe ye that I am able to do this?

FAITH IN THE PROMISES.

THINK of that wonderful rule, "According to thy faith be it unto thee!" Have we not had a private version of the promises something in this wise: "Blessed are they that do hunger and thirst after righteousness, for they shall go on hungering and thirsting"? When we look over our lives, can we not see that according to our faith so it has been unto us? We *have* gone hungering and thirsting; we *have* had just enough strength to labor and not conquer. It is a very different thing to read the Bible with this hidden spirit of mental reservation, or even with the conviction that these have been fulfilled to a favored few, and the firm belief that they will be granted in all their fullness to ourselves individually. Try it but once, and see if it does not seem a new book to you.

Oh, let us pause to think if we *could* but believe God's gracious words, what joy, what confidence would fill our souls! If we could but silence these whispers of distrust, how soon the faith of Paul would bring the peace of Paul into our hearts!

UNTO THEE.

No, not despairingly
  Come I to Thee;
No, not distrustingly
  Bend I the knee.
Sin hath gone over me,
Yet is this still my plea,
  Jesus hath died.

Ah! mine iniquity
  Crimson has been;
Infinite, infinite
  Sin upon sin;

Sin of not loving Thee,
Sin of not trusting Thee,
  Infinite sin.

Lord, I confess to Thee
  Sadly my sin;
All I am, tell I Thee,
  All I have been.
Purge Thou my sin away,
Wash Thou my soul this day,
  Lord, make me clean.

Faithful and just art Thou,
  Forgiving all;
Loving and kind art Thou
  When poor ones call:
Lord, let the cleansing blood,
Blood of the Lamb of God,
  Pass o'er my soul.

Then all is peace and light
  This soul within;
Thus shall I walk with Thee,
  The loved unseen.
Leaning on Thee, my God,
Guided along the road,
  Nothing between.

CHEERFULNESS.

THE faculty of making the most of our blessings is a very happy one. The Spaniard of whom Southey tells that he always put on his magnifying glasses when he ate cherries, in order to make them seem larger, had the true philosophy of life. The good things that fall to the share of most men in this world are not so numerous but that they will bear a little exaggeration, and it is much wiser to make the most of them than to grumble because they are not more numerous. It is surprising how narrow means and simple pleasures may be eked out by a little invention. Sydney Smith, that great master of human happiness, used to cry out, "Glorify the room," and, the windows being thrown open, let in a blaze of sunshine and flowers. The ancient Pompeiians, who were wise in their day and generation, seem to have well understood the art of making the most of everything. Their gardens were very diminutive, but by painting the surrounding walls with plants and landscapes, their little area became indefinitely enlarged to the eye of the observer, just as our shop-keepers enlarge their premises and multiply their goods by the aid of mirrors. It is well to glorify our lives in this way a little by throwing open the windows and taking an enlarged view of all our blessings.

THE PRESENCE OF GOD.

The Christian life should never, can never, be a solitary one; a life of service must be a life of love. And no path can be barren if the fountain of living waters flows by its side. Yet there are lives which bereavement has left very poor in natural companionship, and homes which at times seem silent when the echo of other full and joyous firesides reaches them. And there are those who have no homes on earth, dwelling as strangers in the homes of others; and in all lives there are lonely hours, hours when trial and perplexity come, and the friend on whose sympathy and judgment we would lean is not near; and in many hearts there are places too tender for any human hand to touch.

What a truth, then, is that which turns hours of loneliness into hours of the richest and blessed companionship; companionship which makes the heart glow and the face shine, so that those who dwell much in it bear a visible and sensible sunshine with them wherever they come.

For the presence of God is no abstract truth, no mere presence of a sun, to whose light we may lay open our souls as the flowers their leaves, and be transfigured; but the communion of spirit with spirit; no mere presence of an angel watching us, loving us in silence. It is the presence of One with whom we may have intercourse as a man with his friends; to whom we may speak—speak of everything which interests us; make requests and have them granted, ask questions and have them answered; One who is not silent towards us. Oh, let us bathe ourselves in this joy; drink, yea, drink abundantly of it, and be refreshed! Let us begin every prayer remembering it, and arise from every prayer strengthened with the remembrance; read the Bible as the word of One present; speak of Him as One present; carry it with us all day as our shield and strength, and rest in it all night.

IN THY PRESENCE.

This beautiful hymn was one of the prison songs of Madame Guyon. Her life of exile and imprisonment is a striking illustration of the truth that the believer's happiness is independent of outward events.

> O Thou! by long experience tried,
> Near whom no grief can long abide;
> My Lord, how full of sweet content
> I pass my years of banishment!
>
> All scenes alike engaging prove
> To souls impressed with sacred love!
> Where'er they dwell, they dwell in Thee;
> In heaven, in earth, or on the sea.
>
> To me remains nor place nor time!
> My country is in every clime;
> I can be calm and free from care
> On any shore, since God is there.
>
> While place we seek, or place we shun,
> The soul finds happiness in none;
> But with my God to guide my way,
> 'Tis equal joy to go or stay.
>
> Could I be cast where Thou art not,
> That were indeed a dreadful lot;
> But regions none remote I call,
> Secure of finding God in all.

LIFE'S DRUDGERIES.

If done for Christ, all is grand, the work of spade, of needle, or pen, or sceptre. Let those who are weary of life's lowly duties recall the lines of holy George Herbert:

> "Nothing is so mean,
> Which, when enacted for Thy sake,
>   Will not grow bright and clean.
> A servant with this clause
>   Makes drudgery divine :
> Who sweeps a room as for Thy laws,
>   Makes that and the action fine."

And let it be remembered that God has given His leaders just such training that He has never allowed a man to take a conspicuous place in any department of human society until that man has spent years in unknown, weary, wasting drudgery. In professional, mercantile, social, scientific, political, and military life, He has trained in gloom, and labor, and burden-bearing, and routine drudgery, the men who were to lead the world. So, in the back side of the solitary desert, He trained Moses; so, behind the plough, and among the sheep, and in the fishing-boats, He reared Elisha, and David, and the Disciples. "He that is faithful over a few things shall be made ruler over many," is a principle in His kingdom.

What if no eye sees us, what if no voice praises? At night, when the dull, unappreciated work is over, we can go to Jesus, and meet the glad recognition of His eye, and lay our heads on His shoulder and fall asleep, listening to His voice murmuring the applause of, "Well done! well done! well done!" While we work in alleys and wharves, with drays and carts, in back shops, over saw, or needle, or pen, or in some school of hard, dull children, He is waiting for us, and as we close the door behind us and move, weary and heavy laden, to our homes, He opens His arms and says, "Come to me, come and find rest."

THE CALL.

Come, labor on ;
The laborers are few, the field is wide ;
  New stations must be filled and blanks supplied ;
From voices distant far, or near at home,
    The call is, "Come."

Come, labor on :
The enemy is watching, night and day,
  To sow the tares, to snatch the seed away ;
While we in sleep our duty have forgot,
    He slumbereth not.

Come, labor on ;
Away with gloomy doubt and faithless fear :
  No arm so weak but may do service here :
By feeblest agents can our God fulfil
    His righteous will.

Come, labor on ;
No time for rest, till glows the western sky,
  While the long shadows o'er our pathway lie,
And a glad sound comes with the setting sun,
    "Servants, well done!"

WHAT WE MIGHT HAVE.

"THERE are many gains, many losses in Christ, over and above that great, inappreciable loss of the salvation of the soul in Him. The final aim may be attained, and yet the hearers, who, for love of a great or small possession, depart upon that saying, "Sell that thou hast, and follow me," may have abundant reason for going away sorrowful. We are made poor by what we *miss*, as well as by what we *lose;* a little more patience, a little more consistency, and to what we might not have attained! to what tender intimacy, to what satisfying communications, to what power, what rest, what freedom!"

"THE COMFORTER, WHICH IS THE HOLY GHOST."

> Holy Spirit! Infinite!
> Shine upon our spirit's night
> With Thy blessed inward light,
>   Comforter Divine!

Like the dew Thy peace distil;
Guide, subdue our wayward will;
Things of God revealing still,
  Comforter Divine!

In us, for us, intercede,
And with voiceless yearnings plead
Our unutterable need,
  Comforter Divine!

Search with us the depths of God,
Bear us up the starry road
To the heights of Thine abode,
  Comforter Divine!

EARTHLY CARE HEAVENLY DISCIPLINE.

Suppose, in some bright vision unfolding to our view, in tranquil evening or solemn midnight, the glorified form of some departed friend should appear to us with the announcement, "This year is to be to you one of special probation and discipline, with reference to perfecting you for a heavenly state. Weigh well and consider every incident of your daily life; for not one is to fall out by accident, but each one shall be a finished and indispensable link in a bright chain that is to draw you upward to the skies."

With what new eyes should we now look on our daily lot! and if we found in it not a single change—the same old cares, the same perplexities, the same uninteresting drudgeries, still—with what new meaning would every incident be invested, and with what other and sublimer spirit could we meet them? Yet, if announced by one rising from the dead, with the visible glory of a spiritual world, this truth could be asserted no more clearly and distinctly than Jesus Christ has stated it already. Not a sparrow falleth to the ground, without our Father—not one of them is forgotten by Him; and we are of more value than many sparrows—yea, even the hairs of our head are all numbered. Not till the belief in these declarations in their most literal sense, becomes the calm and settled habit of the soul, is life ever redeemed from drudgery and dreary emptiness, and made full of interest, meaning, and divine significance. Not till then do its grovelling wants, its wearying cares, its stinging vexations, become to us ministering spirits—each one, by a silent but certain agency fitting us for a higher and perfect sphere.

OUR PRIVILEGE.

THE disciples of John were in great trouble. They were perplexed and cast down, and knew not what to do. In their difficulties they went and told Jesus. It was His cause. He was able to comfort them, and He knew what to do.

We are often in trouble. We are often in doubt. What we ought to do is not plain to us. We are disposed, at such times, to seek counsel of a friend — to lean upon a human arm. But it is our privilege to go directly to Jesus. Everything affecting His disciples concerns Him. Nothing is beneath His care or notice. If troubles come, He knows how to comfort us. If difficulties arise, He can lead us through them. If we are perplexed and cast down, He can lift us up and make our way plain. We need not wait for great trials or troubles, but go to Him with all the little things of every-day life. He loves to go with His disciples everywhere, and be with them at all times. He is thus an all-sufficient Saviour— an ever-present help in every time of need.

The *habit* of telling Jesus everything is of itself an incalculable blessing. The effect of thus telling Him brings us into His immediate presence, and is the greatest possible safeguard and protection.

THE BURDEN LAID DOWN.

What is it to cast the care on God?
Is it to keep the heaviest load,
 And lay some trifling weight aside?
Still taking thought for every hour,
As if the Lord's sustaining power
 Were still unknown—at least untried.

Is it to shrink at future things,
To start at what the present brings,
 And groan when we but feel the rod?
Not to rejoice till we receive,
And only when we see believe;
 Is this to cast the care on God?

No, the believer doth not so;
As Shiloh's waters softly go,
 He keeps his straight and even way,
No evil tidings doth he fear,
His heart is fixed, his help is near,
 His strength is equal to his day.

Onward he presses for the crown,
He lays his heavy burden down,
 A weight the pilgrim cannot bear;
His foes without, his fears within,
His griefs, his weakness, and his sin,
 And everything that causeth care.

Should doubts arise, should ills betide,
"God will protect, God will provide,"
　　He saith, and pondering in his breast,
　The promise of his faithful Lord,
　He still believes His plighted word,
　　And so he "enters into rest."

NO EXCUSE.

"Sleep not away thy time for prayer in the morning, and then think thou art sufficiently excused for omitting it, because thy worldly business calls thee another way. Jade not thy body with overlaboring, nor overcharge thy mind with too heavy a load of worldly cares in the day, and then think the weariness of the one, and discomposure of the other, will discharge thee from praying at night; this is to make a sin thy apology for neglecting a duty.

OUR EARTHLY TIES

Let us count up our treasures of kindred; they are our best. Let us "consider" them in the presence of our Father in heaven. Is there any tie which absence has loosened, or which the wear and tear of every-day intercourse, little uncongenialities, unconfessed misunderstandings, have fretted into the heart until it bears something of the nature of a fetter? Any relationship we have not fully realized for want of dwelling on it? Any cup at our home table whose sweetness we have not fully tasted, though it might yet make of our daily bread a continual feast?

Let us reckon up these treasures now whilst they are still ours, in thankfulness to God. Let us not first learn how large a space of the heart they fill, and might fill with grateful joy, by finding how large a space they have left empty. Let us extend the circle of our relationships wide, beyond the home, from those ties of kindred so close when strengthened by early associations *within* the home, to those whose connection with us God regards as no loose, mechanical bond, but as one of His appointed relationships, placing servants and masters in the next ring of the circle to parents and children; for there is one feature in all human relationships on which we can none of us bear to dwell; yet, if we could let the heart gaze on for a moment, whilst they are yet ours, we might give ourselves and others much more joy, and spare ourselves much of life's very bitterest sorrow—the thought of what might have been. They cannot last forever. One by one they must be severed; and at last we must be severed from them all. Tightly, tenderly, let us bind these blessed ties around our hearts. Let not their strength be first felt as they are broken; let not our first conscious clinging to our beloved be the convulsive clinging of those who must part. Now, now, let us learn the full worth of our human relationships, counting over, as the veriest misers, the full amount of this, our best wealth, that we may use it and enjoy it richly as God would have us; for we are disciples, not of him who was in the wilderness until the day of his showing to Israel, but of Him who, before His ministry as the Christ of God began, dwelt for thirty years with His mother in the home of Nazareth, who has given us, as the deepest name of heaven, "My Father's House," and as the dearest title of the Church, the "Family of God."

INTERRUPTIONS IN OUR WORK.

WE are too much wedded to our plans, whether they be plans for a life, or plans for a day or an hour; too little loyal at heart to the will of God. And hence arise great uneasiness and discomposure of mind, which, from whatever source it arises, cannot fail to be prejudicial and a hindrance to the spiritual life. We have set apart, it may be, such an hour of the day for the purpose of devotion or study. But just as we were about to spend it so, some call of necessity or charity, arises in another direction. In either case, whether it be of necessity or charity it is God's call; and not our duty only, but our happiness, lies in responding to it cheerfully and lovingly. We must be ready to go out of our way if God calls us out of our way, or, in other words, to have our little plans so modified and corrected as to be brought into the scheme of His great and all-wise plan. It is every way better to do what God intends for us than what we intend for ourselves.

———

GROWTH IN GRACE.

Grow in grace; because this is the only way to be certain that you have any grace at all. If we aim not at growth in grace, we have never been converted to goodness. He that is satisfied with his attainments has attained nothing. He that sees so little of the promises of the inward, transforming, elevating influences of grace, as to think that he has attained all he can desire, has never understood the first elements of the Christian life. No! we are begotten to a life which aspires after perfection; we have desires awakened which nothing but complete holiness will satisfy. He who says he is content with his progress has never set out to heaven.

SELF-KNOWLEDGE.

This did not once so trouble me,
That better I could not love Thee,
But now I feel and know

That only when we love, we find
How far our hearts remain behind
　　The love they should bestow.

While we had little care to call
On Thee, and scarcely prayed at all,
　　We seemed enough to pray ;
But now we only think with shame
How seldom to Thy glorious name
　　Our lips their offerings pay.

And when we gave yet slighter heed
Unto our brother's suffering need,
　　Our hearts reproached us then
Not half so much as now, that we
With such a careless eye can see
　　The woes and wants of men.

In doing is this knowledge won,
To see what yet remains undone ;
　　With this our pride repress ;
And give us grace, a growing store,
That day by day we may do more,
　　And may esteem it less.

ENCOURAGEMENT TO PRAYER.

We may be too bold in our manner of approach to God, but we cannot be too bold in our expectations from Him. "He that spared not His own Son, but delivered Him up for us all, how shall He not with Him also *freely give us all things.*" What other pledge, what more encouragement can we need, why we should not draw nigh with the largest desire and the most heavenly expectations? The act of prayer will increase the power to pray; while the enjoyment realized in the effect of prayer will stamp the duty as our highest privilege, as the support of our daily and hourly life, support, and consolation.

Instead, therefore, of saying, "We have nothing to draw with, and the well is deep," let us try what faith can do, and with joy shall we draw water out of the wells of salvation. Let us bring our empty vessels until not one is left. Yes, believer, there is indeed a bountiful supply of grace—of every kind—suited to every want; grace to pardon, grace to quicken, grace to bless. Oh, see then that you come not empty away! Remember who it is that pleads before the throne. Remember that the grace you need is at hand. From eternity He foreknew your case. He laid your portion by. He has kept it for the time of need, and now he only waits for an empty vessel into which to pour His supply. He is ready to show you how infinitely His grace exceeds all thoughts, all prayers, all desires, all praises.

TRUST TO HIS GUIDING.

"Speak unto the children of Israel, that they go forward."

THERE are times in every Christian's life when his way seems hedged up, he hardly knows where to turn. If his earthly affairs are getting bad, or his children are giving him trouble, or sickness is filling him with pain and weariness, his heart will sometimes sink, and fear and despondency make him miserable.

Or if his sins and infirmities, which he has been struggling against ever since he called Jesus, Master, for a while seem to have new power and to overcome him, he at times almost gives up hope, and thinks that he has been mistaken and is not a real Christian.

Or if long months or years he has been kept from active life and work, and made to suffer in secret, away from the observation of good men, and not permitted to go to church or labor in the Sunday-school or other Christian fields, at times his hope and his heart fail him, and he cries out with David, "My tears have been my meat day and night, while they continually say unto me, Where is thy God?"

Satan has much to do with these frames and feelings, and God permits much in the Christian's life and way that is strange and mysterious. We cannot explain or understand it; but one thing we know, that He has said, "I will never leave thee or forsake thee," and in our calmer moments and brighter days we shall believe that He is leading us in the best way.

We have nothing to do with results, they are in His hands. We are to go forward in the path He has evidently marked out for us. It cannot be more hedged up or fearful than was the condition of the Israelites when they stood with the Red Sea on one side, and the hosts of Pharaoh on the other. Jesus gave to Moses and his people on that day a great deliverance, and He will deliver you; and no one who loves Him is so poor, or sick, or weary, or sinful, or helpless, or troubled, but that he shall be kept by His mighty power, and be gathered within His fold, safe from storms and tempests, where no sorrow or sin can crush the heart, and where "the inhabitant shall not say, I am sick."

"THE DARKNESS HIDETH NOT FROM THEE."

Is the night blackness? doth each star
    Refuse upon thy way to shine?
How strong thy consolations are!
    The hand that leads thee is divine;
God waiteth for no guiding ray,
To Him the night shines as the day;
    It is not dark to the Lord.

Are the mists heavy? closing round
    Thy pilgrim road on every side?
Life drawn within that narrow bound,
    The world beyond forlornly wide?
Poor weary child, are thine eyes dim?
Trust thyself wholly then to Him:
    It is not dark to the Lord.

Are the clouds thickening? covering all
   Thy little spot of fair blue sky?
Do the great drops begin to fall,
   And winds and lightnings round thee fly?
Look unto Jesus: fear no more
To follow where He goes before:
   It is not dark to the Lord.

THE MORNING HOUR.

The importance of the morning hour cannot be overrated. That the period immediately after rising should be scrupulously consecrated to God, that the earliest thoughts of the day should be filled with God, that the homage of self-dedication should be renewed before starting on another pilgrimage, that we should listen to His small voice of warning and encouragement as it issues from the pages of His written word—all this is so essentially bound up with the peace and holiness of the day, that one might almost say the two are inseparable.

The tone of sentiment and feeling maintained throughout the day is sure to take its coloring from that morning hour.

SPIRITUAL DEPRESSION.

When Satan comes with his suggestions of doubt, meet him with more positive assertions of your faith than ever you have made before. I say, when Satan comes, because all doubts are from him, and all discouragements also. The Holy Spirit never suggests a thought of doubt or discouragement to any soul. Never! Settle this matter once for all, and you will find the way wonderfully cleared. Your doubts, then, are all from Satan, and you know he has been a liar from the beginning. Do not give heed to them for a moment. . . . Consecrate your power of believing to the Lord Jesus just as you have consecrated all your other powers, and trust Him to keep you trusting. Let nothing shake your faith. Should even sin unhappily overtake you, still you must not doubt. At once, on the discovery of it, take 1 John i. 9, and act on it: "If we confess our sins, He is faithful and just to forgive us our sins, and to cleanse us from *all* unrighteousness." Confess your sin, therefore, immediately upon the discovery of it, and believe at once that God does forgive it, and does again cleanse you from all unrighteousness; and go on believing it. Believe it more firmly than ever. Believe it, because He says it, and not because you feel it or see it. Believe it whether you feel it or not. Believe it even when it seems to you that you are believing something that is absolutely untrue. Believe it actively and persistently, and according to your faith it shall be unto you.

ABOVE ALL, THE SHIELD.

FAITH fails ;
Then in the dust
Lie failing rest, and light, and trust.
So doth the troubled soul itself distress,
And choke the fountain in the wilderness.
I care not what your peace assails !
The deep root is : faith fails.

Faith fails ;
When in the breast
The Lord's sweet presence doth not rest ;
For who believes, clouds cannot make afraid ;
He knows the sun doth shine behind the shade ;
He rides at anchor through the gales.
Do you not so ? faith fails.

Faith fails ;
Its foes alarm,
And persecution's threats disarm ;
False friends can scarcely wish it a good-day,
Before it taketh fright and shrinks away.
When God doth guard, what foe prevails !
Why then the fear ? faith fails.

Faith fails ;
Else cares would die,
And we should on God's care rely.

Man for the coming day doth grieve and fret,
And all past days doth sinfully forgot.
For every beast God's care avails,
Why not for us? faith fails.

   Faith fails;
Then cometh fears.
If sickness comes, if death is near,
O man, why is it when the times are bad,
And the days evil, that thy face is sad?
How is it that thy courage quails?
It must be this : faith fails.

   My God!
Let my faith be
Living or working actively,
With hope and joy, that death may not surprise ;
So let them sweetly close my eyes.
The Christian's *life* to death may yield ;
Hope stands, faith has the field.

LIFT UP YOUR HEARTS.

Do you ever use ejaculatory prayer? Do you ever lift up your heart to God in the midst of your work, praying Him to shield you from temptation, to bless you in what you are doing, and, at all events, not to let you wander very far from His side? Do not say it is impossible; for to this and no lower standard you are called, both by the constitution of your nature, and by the precept, "Pray without ceasing;" and by the grace of God all things which He commands are possible. You will say, perhaps, "I try to keep my mind continually in the right track; but alas! it is thrown off its balance a thousand times a day, by having to do things in a hurry and against time; by a warm conversation; by a piece of interesting news; by domestic worries and cares; by little rubs of temper." So it is most truly. The mind wants steadying and setting right many times a day. It resembles a compass placed on a rickety table; the least stir of the table makes the needle swing round and point untrue. Let it settle, then, till it points aright. Be perfectly silent for a few moments, thinking of JESUS; there is an almost divine force in silence. Drop the thing that worries, that excites, that interests, that thwarts you; let it fall, like a sediment, to the bottom, until the soul is no longer turbid; and say secretly: "Grant, I beseech Thee, merciful Lord, to thy faithful servant pardon and peace; that I may be cleansed from all my sins, and serve Thee with a *quiet mind.*" Yes! with a quiet mind. We cannot serve Him with a turbid one; it is a mere impossibility. Thus composing ourselves from time to time, thus praying, and setting the mind's needle true, we shall little by little approximate towards that devout frame which binds the soul to its true centre, even while it travels through worldly business, worldly excitements, worldly cares.

———

CHRIST A REFUGE.

"A man shall be as a hiding-place from the wind, and a covert from the tempest."

Our refuge, if we will but enter it, is always as near to us as our danger; it is sometimes nearer. There, but a little way off, comes the overwhelming storm; but here, not a little way off, close to us, at our right hand, within one step of us, is our hiding-place. The happy psalmist well knew this. "God is our refuge and strength," he says; not a present, but a "very present help in trouble." Speaking of the Church, he says again, not "God is near her," but, "God is in the midst of her; she shall not be moved; God shall help her, and that right early." There is no casting out of any one who is hid in Christ; there is no keeping out of any one who wishes to hide himself in Him. And it does not matter what the evil is we wish to escape. There is as good shelter in Him from what we deem a small danger as from a great one, and we are as welcome to come to Him for it. He is as much a refuge for an aching or careworn or fearful heart, as for a perishing, guilty soul. He is a hiding-place from every wind, a covert from every tempest.

FROM SELF TO CHRIST.

MANY timid followers of the Lord, with broken health and shattered nerves, add to their own sorrows the often-recurring thought that they have grievously departed from God. They have lost some of the comforts which they enjoyed in other days, and thus they think it was better with them then than now. The overtaxed brain, the jaded mind, and weary body cannot respond to the joy that once thrilled their souls at thoughts of the Lord's gracious dealings with them.

Distrust not His love, thou tried and tempted one. Jesus is the *same*. Thy heart is resting on Him, or it would not grieve over its own unworthiness, and that it can no longer offer the glad sacrifice of praise. Christ is all, all that you cannot be, and He is thy praise. Fear not! His thoughts are "thoughts of peace, and not of evil." Another thorn in the chaplet will make heaven the sweeter. Soon shall the thorns be exchanged for a crown of glory, and the sight of Him thou lovest shall make amends for all.

LOVE'S MYSTERY.

Care and labor manifold
   Have wearied me all day;
I have no thought or language,
   I have no strength to pray.

But Jesus knows I love him,
　Though not a word I say.

The tempter hath beguiled me ;
　Earth sought mine ear to win ;
Alas ! I cannot answer
　How I have let them in.
But Jesus knows I love Him,
　And hate my heart of sin.

The tempter will accuse me,
　And death shall come one day ;
Justice, with fearful charges,
　And I no debt can pay.
But Jesus knows I love Him
　When I have naught to say.

I have no voice to praise Him,
　I have no eyes to see ;
But full of hallelujahs
　My silent soul must be.
For Jesus knows I love Him,
　Without one word from me.

O Justice ! dread avenger !
　O death, in Justice' name !
Where are your boasted triumphs?
　Your terrors are in vain—

For I know that Jesus loves me!
All praise to His dear name!

WATCHING UNTO PRAYER.

"I prevented the dawning of the morning, and cried: I hoped in thy Word. Mine eyes prevent the night watches, that I might meditate in thy Word."

WHEN the heart is really engaged for God, time will always be found for secret duties, and rather will be redeemed, as with David, from sleep, than lost from prayer. And when we see a man, like the king of Israel, engaged in the most active employments of life, yet, "sanctifying" such frequent seasons, in the short period of each successive day, "with the Word of God and prayer," we cannot want a clearer evidence of the insincerity of the excuse that professes that no time can be spared from the pressing avocations of the day, for the service of God. It is not that such men are busy, and have *no time* for prayer; but that they are worldly, and have *no heart* to pray.

THE POWER OF THE CROSS OF CHRIST.

They were living to themselves; self, with its hopes, and promises, and dreams, had still hold of them; but He began to fulfil their prayers. They had asked for contrition, and He sent them sorrow; they had asked for purity, and he sent them thrilling anguish; they had asked to be meek, and He had broken their hearts; they had asked to be dead to the world, and He slew all their living hopes; they had asked to be made like unto Him, and He placed them in the furnace, sitting by "as a refiner of silver," till they should reflect His image. They had asked to lay hold of His cross, and when He reached it to them it lacerated their hands; they had asked they knew not what, nor how; but He had taken them at their word, and granted them all their petitions. They were hardly willing to follow on so far, or to draw so nigh to Him. They had upon them an awe and fear, as Jacob at Bethel, or Eliphaz in the night visions, or as the apostles when they thought they had seen a spirit, and knew not that it was Jesus. They could almost pray Him to depart from them, or to hide His awfulness. They found it easier to obey than to suffer—to do than to give up —to bear the cross than to hang upon it: but they cannot go back, for they have come too near the unseen cross, and its virtues have pierced too deeply within them. He is fulfilling to them His promise, "And I, if I be lifted up, will draw all men unto me:" but now *their* turn is come at last. Before, they had only *heard* of the mystery, but now they *feel* it. He has fastened on them His look of love, as He did on Mary and Peter, and they cannot choose but follow. Little by little, from time to time, by flitting gleams, the mystery of His cross shines out upon them. They behold Him lifted up, and the glory which rays forth from the wounds of His holy passion: and as they gaze upon it, they advance, and are changed into His likeness, and His name shines out through them, for He dwells in them. They live alone with Him above, in unspeakable fellowship: willing to lack what others own, and to be unlike all, so that they are only like Him. Such are they in all ages who follow the Lamb whithersoever He goeth. Had they chosen for themselves, or their friends chosen for them, they would have chosen otherwise. They would have been brighter here, but less glorious in His kingdom. They would have had Lot's portion, not Abraham's, if they had halted anywhere—

if He had taken off His hand and let them stray back—and what would they not have lost? What forfeits in the morning of the resurrection! But He stayed them up, even against themselves. Many a time their foot had well-nigh slipped. But He in mercy held them up: now, even in this life, they know all He did was done well. It was good for them to stand alone with Him on the mountain, and in the cloud, and that not their will, but His, was done on them.

IN THE FIELD.

Fighting the Battle of Life!
   With a weary heart and head,
For in the midst of the strife
   The banners of Joy are fled—
Fled and gone out of sight,
   When I thought they were so near—
And the music of Hope, this night,
   Is dying away on my ear.

FOR DAILY LIFE.

Fighting the whole day long!
    With a very tired hand—
With only my armor strong
    The shelter in which I stand.
There is nothing left of me—
    If all my strength were shown,
So small the amount would be
Its presence could scarce be known.

Fighting alone to-night,
    With not even a stander-by
To cheer me in the fight,
    Or to hear me when I cry.
Only the Lord can hear,
    Only the Lord can see
The struggle within how dark and drear,
    Though quiet the outside be.

Fighting alone to-night!
    With what a sinking heart;
Lord Jesus, in the fight,
    Oh, stand not Thou apart!
Body and mind have tried
    To make the field my own,
But when the Lord is on my side,
    He doeth the work alone.

And when He hideth His face,
   And the battle-clouds prevail,
It is only through His grace
   If I do not utterly fail.
The word of old was true,
   And its truth shall never cease:
" The Lord shall fight for you,
   And ye shall hold your peace."

Lord, I would fain be still
   And quiet behind my shield;
But make me to love Thy will,
   For fear I should ever yield.
For when to destroy my foes,
   Thou lettest them strike at me,
And fillest my heart with woes,
   That joy may the purer be,—

Nothing but perfect trust,
   And love of Thy perfect will,
Can raise me out of the dust,
   And bid my fears be still.
Even as now my hands,
   So doth my folded will
Lie waiting Thy commands,
   Without one anxious thrill.

But as with sudden pain
    My hands unfold and clasp,
So doth my will start up again,
    And taketh its old firm grasp.
Lord, fix my eyes upon Thee,
    And fill my heart with Thy love,
And keep my soul till the shadows flee,
    And the light breaks forth above.

FRAGMENTS OF TIME.

IN order to achieve some good work which you have much at heart, you may not be able to secure an entire week or even an uninterrupted day. But try what you can make of the broken fragments of time. Glean up its golden dust—those reapings and parings of precious duration—those leavings of days, and remnants of hours, which soon may sweep out into the waste of existence. And thus, if you be a miser of moments—if you be frugal, and hoard up odd minutes and half hours and unexpected holidays — your careful gleanings may eke out a long and useful life, and you may die at last richer in existence than multitudes whose time is all their own. The time which some men waste in superfluous slumbers, and idle visits, and desultory application, were it all redeemed, would give them wealth of leisure, and enable them to execute undertakings for which they deem a less worried life than theirs essential. When a person says, "I have no time to pray, no time to read the Bible, no time to improve my mind, or to do a kind turn to a neighbor," he may be saying what he thinks, but he should not think what he says; for if he has not got the time already, he may get it by redeeming it.

READ WITH PRAYER.

The Holy Spirit alone can make us feel the things which are easy to be understood, and prevent our wresting those which are hard.

Never, then, should the Bible be opened except with prayer for the teachings of this Spirit.

You will read without profit as long as you read without prayer. It is only in the degree that the Spirit, which indited a text, takes it from the page and breathes it into the heart, that we can comprehend its meaning, be touched by its beauty, stirred by its remonstrance, or animated by its promises.

AVOID ANXIETY.

An anxious mind is never a holy mind.

THE BEAUTY OF HOLINESS.

Do you recollect the expression, "The beauty of holiness?" I have looked at many men in my life, who were stern, and proud, and reliable, and sound in truth, and sturdily good, and have wondered as I looked at them, whether the thought ever crossed their mind, "What is the meaning of the *beauty of holiness?*" and whether it ever occurred to them that God wanted divine qualities among men interpreted so as to make them attractive as well as useful.

That which is true in respect to the exhibition of moral traits, is true in respect to the performance of the whole round of Christian duties. We can take up our cross every day and leave the impression that we are more unholy than before we became Christians. I think persons, after becoming Christians, sometimes seem to be more selfish than when they made no profession of religion. There is such a thing as spiritual selfishness. If a person is so wrapped up in religious self-contemplation as to forget those around about him, he is spiritually selfish. At any rate, many persons who leave their evil ways, and attempt to become better men, create the feeling among their associates that they have lost warmth; that they have deteriorated in social elements: that they are not as engaging as they were. "They may be safer," it is said, "but they have sold their beauty to get grace."

Now, I hold that every man who becomes a Christian is bound to glorify God in his conduct. He is bound to illustrate the beauty of religion. He is bound to let his light so shine that men shall be drawn to holiness of life, and not be repelled from it. He is bound to make the sanctuary where he has invested his heart, seem like a paradise to those about him.

LORD, HERE AM I.

Still, as of old, Thy precious word
Is by the nations dimly heard:
The hearts its holiness hath stirred
    Are weak and few.
Wise men the secret dare not tell;
Still in Thy temple slumbers well
Good Eli: Oh, like Samuel,
    Lord, here am I!

Few powers, no wisdom, no renown,
Only my life can I lay down,
Only my heart, Lord, to Thy throne
    I bring, and pray
That, child of Thine, I may go forth,
And spread glad tidings through the earth,
And teach sad hearts to know Thy worth;
    Lord, here am I!

Weak lips may teach the wise, Christ said;
Weak feet sad wanderers home have led;
Weak hands have cheered the sick one's bed
    With freshest flowers;

O teach me, Father! heed their sighs,
While many a soul in darkness lies
And waits Thy message; make me wise.
    Lord, here am I!

I ask no heaven till earth be Thine,
Nor glory-crown while work of mine
Remaineth here; when earth shall shine
    Among the stars,
Her sins wiped out, her captives free,
Her voice a music unto Thee,—
For crown, new work give Thou to me!
    Lord, here am I!

REST IN THE LORD.

MANY of the children of God hope to be saved, and yet do not enjoy that true satisfaction and restfulness of spirit which they might. It is often because they look for happiness separate from Jesus, or allow themselves to be distressed and anxious about all the difficulties and trials of life, instead of committing every one, small as well as great, to the Lord, and then resting upon Him, waiting patiently for Him. "Thou wilt keep him in perfect peace whose mind is stayed on Thee, because he TRUSTETH in Thee." It is the feeling of the little child who nestles in its father's arms, knowing that nowhere else is it so happy or so secure; and if it leaves this safe retreat for lessons or for play, it is still happy and contented in the consciousness that the parent's love is ever around it, providing for every want and ready to sympathize with every trouble. For the soul may rest on the Lord, while all the powers of mind and body are actively employed in His service.

STEPS TO HOLINESS.

WHAT does growing in grace mean, but that this spiritual intention should lengthen its reach—should extend itself more and more to every corner of our life? Some little business of routine calls my attention at a certain hour, having nothing sublime or extraordinary in it, but the neglect of which would entail discomfort and annoyance—a visit, or a letter of courtesy, or an interview, in which a few necessary words pass, and then it is over. Well; even the most earthly of earthly actions, those which are most bound up with this transitory state of things, and which have no intrinsic dignity or sacredness whatever, may be spiritualized by importing into them a spiritual intention. The little courtesies, for example, which society requires, may be yielded simply because they *are* social requirements, in which case they will be often done "grudgingly, and of necessity;" or they may be regarded as so many opportunities of compliance with the inspired precept, "Be courteous"—in which case they will be done cheerfully, "as to the

Lord, and not unto men." And (generally) the meeting all calls upon us, however humble, with the thought that they come to us in the way of God's providence, and in the working out of the system of things which He has appointed, and are indications of the quarter in which He would have us direct our energies, is a great means of purifying our intention, and so of advancing us in spirituality. For nobody is aware what is going on in our hearts, when we meet these calls in a devout spirit; our friends only see us doing common-place things which others do, and give us no credit. But, in so meeting such calls, we have praise of God, who, like a good father, marks with a smile of approbation the humblest efforts of His children to please Him.

SINGLENESS OF PURPOSE.

By this is meant that every end proposed should be simply and solely for good, for the glory of God. And this same singleness of purpose is to be carried into every department of life. God and His glory are to stand first. Everything is to be shaped and directed with reference to this. We are to do nothing, go nowhere, enter upon no enterprise without first asking God's direction, and without considering whether we ought to do it. Our inclinations and wishes will not be a safe guide. These we may have to give up. There is something higher and nobler than the mere gratification of our wishes. But in putting duty first we shall never suffer loss.

CHRIST'S SERVICE AND OURS.

Oh what a picture of devotedness does His lowly service present to us! Look at

Him beginning His course, knowing each sorrow that was to befall Him; foreseeing the whole course of rejection, and the shameful end of His pilgrimage; rejected, when He would minister blessing; misunderstood, when He gave instruction; suffering not merely at the hands of enemies, but more acutely from those around Him; to them alone He said, "How long shall I suffer you?"—rejected, misunderstood, suffering, He goes forward without the slightest faltering; He never stops for a moment in His devoted service to all around Him. To the very end of His course, as at the beginning, He is the meat of all who need and will accept Him. We think when trouble or sorrow comes on us, that it is time to care for ourselves. Not so Jesus. We think there must be a limit to our self-sacrifice. Not so our blessed Lord. We think that our interests, our credit, or at least our life, must not be touched or endangered. We think when our kindness is rejected, we need not repeat it. We think our times of rest and relaxation are our own. Oh, how unlike to us in all was our blessed, lowly Master! Oh, how far above us in all things! Nothing moved His steadfast heart, or turned Him from doing good. In vain was the stupidity of His disciples, the rage of His enemies, or the craft of Satan. Jesus never wavered nor hesitated; His course of self-surrender was complete.

REJOICE! REJOICE!

"*He hath given us all things richly to enjoy.*"

The love of nature, and the power
   To read her glowing page;
The pleasure of each passing hour,
   In youth or riper age;
The buoyant, bounding pulse of health;
   The strength for duty's task;
Bright thoughts and garnered mental wealth,

More than thy soul didst ask ;
These are the gifts of God—Rejoice, rejoice !

The hope of better things to come,
 Of higher joys in store ;
The vision of a brighter home
 Where change shall vex no more ;
All that the present brings to thee
 Of blessings in their bloom ;
All that the great eternity
 Can yield beyond the tomb ;
These are the gifts of God—Rejoice, rejoice !

ST. PAUL'S THREE PSALMS OF THANKSGIVING.

First for the gift of a Saviour—"Thanks be unto God for his unspeakable gift."

Second for triumph through that Saviour over every trial, temptation and sin,—

"Thanks be to God which always causeth us to triumph in Christ."

And lastly, for victory over death through the same gracious Saviour, who "with His own right hand and holy arm hath gotten Himself the victory," to give it unto His people,—

"THANKS BE TO GOD, which giveth us the victory, through our Lord Jesus Christ."

A MOTIVE FOR CHRISTIAN WORK.

As we read the sublime verses in the latter part of the 15th chapter of 1st Corinthians, commencing, "Behold, I show you a mystery: We shall not all sleep, but we shall all be changed," etc., on to the words "Thanks be to God which giveth us the victory, through our Lord Jesus Christ," and then think of our daily struggles with temptation and trials, caused by our own sins, and the evil that is in the world, we are ready to exclaim, "Oh that we could leave it all and go now to the enjoyment of this victory in the presence of Christ and His redeemed in glory." But as we read the verse which follows, we see that it was not to awaken longings such as these that the promise of victory in the last conflict was given, but rather to animate us to zeal and earnestness in the work which Christ has given us to do here on the earth.

"*Therefore,*" because you have these precious promises, "my beloved brethren, be ye steadfast, unmoveable, always abounding in the work of the Lord, forasmuch as ye know that your labour is not in vain in the Lord."

TILL HE COME.

"Till He come"—oh! let the words
  Linger on the trembling chords;
Let the "little while" between
  In their golden light be seen;
Let us think how heaven and home
Lie beyond that "Till He come."

When the weary ones we love
Enter on their rest above,
Seems the earth so poor and vast,
All our life-joy overcast?

Hush, be every murmur dumb;
It is only—" Till He come."

Clouds and conflicts round us press;
Would we have one sorrow less?
All the sharpness of the cross,
All that tells the world is loss,
Death and darkness and the tomb
Only whisper " Till He come."

See the feast of love is spread;
Drink the wine, and break the bread,
Sweet memorials, till the Lord
Call us round His heavenly board,
Some from earth, from glory some,
Sever'd only—" Till He come."

LEARNING THE LESSON.

THE believer, as he advances in self-knowledge, learns to bless and to adore those piercing yet enlightening experiences of his own weakness which, as it were, let daylight within his whole spiritual being. He learns, even in exclaiming, " Who shall deliver me from the body of this death?" to rejoice in those, its deep-seated infirmities, against which he continually prays and strives; he finds many things within him, pitiable rather than sinful; hindrances from which he longs to free himself, yet learns even in these to recognize his true though humble friends and helpers; *him they compel to bear the cross;* and even in that compulsory bearing, his heart so grows to it as to desire no independent strength or virtue. "Blessed are ye poor." Blessed are the souls in whom not the strength of nature only, but that of grace, has been brought so low, even to the very dust, that they have learned to call nothing that they have their own.

Often must the believer, like Antæus, grow stronger for having touched the ground; often must he experience the sentence of death *in himself;* must feel himself a being without heart or hope, incapable and even insensible, so that he may learn to trust, not in himself, or any other, but in Him who raises the spiritually dead. The Christian must hold on to God through conflicts and agonies; he must fight while the blood runs down and glues his hand to his sword, so must he hold on when that hand is benumbed and stiff with cold; when strength and consciousness seem gone together, and only an instinct remains through which the soul is able to fling itself like a dead weight upon Christ. Yet even here is

——"an overthrow,
Worth many victories."

Through being chilled and mortified in the smallest, most inwardly humiliating things; through being beaten away from the broken cisterns of self and of all creatures, we learn, as we could never without this have done, to look to Christ as our well of life, and so to find *all* our fresh springs in Him, as to be able to say with a simple and sincere heart: "Lord, give me evermore of this water, so that I thirst not, neither come hither to draw."

FRESH SPRINGS.

"All my Fresh Springs shall be in Thee."

Why is the world so thirsty,
   So restless, ill at ease,
So careworn with its pleasures,
   So difficult to please?
Because the truth it cannot see,
That all "fresh springs" must be in THEE!

Why is Thy Church so weary?
   Why does Thy cherished Bride
Appear so sad and lonely,
   So far from "satisfied"?
What once she knew, she fails to see,
That all her "fresh springs" are in THEE!

Why needs she so much urging
   To work, and love, and feel?
Why craves she fresh excitement
   To stimulate her zeal?

She cannot, or she will not, see
That all "fresh springs" must be in THEE.

Too true it is! On every side
We look in vain for Christ's true Bride!
We hardly recognize her now,
So faint the glory on her brow!
She lives an outside life—not void
Of talents usefully employed.
The tilted vessel overflows,
But day by day more empty grows;
Too seldom is it filled with care,
By meditation and by prayer,
For Christ's own Bride—how strange to own!—
Is seldom with her Lord alone!

Is it not strange! With what surprise
Must it be seen by angel eyes!
But that my own deceitful heart
In all these scenes has borne a part,
The sad reality would seem
The groundless terror of a dream!

I should have thought that she would prize
The mute appeal of those kind eyes,
The incommunicable things
Which JESUS CHRIST's own Presence brings,

The sight of the Incarnate Son,
Unseen yet fondly gazed upon,
The speaking silence in Him found,
The wordless voice, " 'Tis holy ground :"

Yes, verily, I should have thought,
Unless by sad experience taught,
That such exceeding tenderness,
Such all-surpassing loveliness,
Once seen and tasted, had sufficed
To make her lose herself in Christ!

I should have thought that one so blest
Would never care to leave her nest,
Unless, on wings of love, to fly,
Led by the glances of His eye,
And, keeping Him in sight, fulfil
Some fresh expression of His will :
Then, home returning at His call,
Come straight to Him, and tell Him all
Confess her failures on His breast,
Give Him the glory of the rest,
And then, with loving heart and true,
Ask what He next would have her do ;
The passion of her heart fulfilled,
If all be done as He hath willed :

His thoughts, the standard of her own,
His Will, life's sweetest undertone,
No work of love too great, or small
To undertake at His dear call!

 I should have thought the favored Bride
Would cling forever to His side,
And need no pressure of alarm
To make her lean upon His Arm;
No sudden or extreme distress,
To prove His glorious faithfulness;
No failure of all earthly things,
To drive her to the heavenly springs.

 I should have thought she would not care
For any joy He did not share,
Nor any earthly object prize
If Jesus did not sympathize;
Nor let herself be "greatly moved"
By human blame, if He approved;
Nor have a single plan apart
From Him, the Sovereign of her heart;
But hang upon His every word,
And treasure up each accent heard,
Each tone of love, each—less than tone,
Each look of love that said: "Mine own!"

And never, never turn away
From so much love, and coldly say :
" I have not time for Thee to-day !"

O Jesus ! Wondrous, loving Lord !
Untired still ! Be Thou adored !
Thy patience with Thy fickle Bride
May well attract her to Thy side !
Oh ! that she may Thy whisper hear,
" Return ! Return ! For I am near !"
And ever henceforth taste and see
That all her fresh springs are in Thee !

UNTO HIM WHO LOVES US.

O BLESSED Saviour, whose love to sinners passeth the comprehension of men and of angels, and will be the theme of grateful praise throughout the ages of eternity: impress upon us, we beseech Thee, such a deep and abiding sense of our indebtedness for Thy great salvation, that we may wholly live to Thy glory, and serve Thee in holiness and righteousness all our days, until we join in the songs of Thy redeemed army in heaven, where, with the Father and the Holy Ghost, Thou art worshipped and glorified, world without end. *Amen.*

INDEX.

	PAGE
All Things are Yours.........ANNA L. WARING.	16
Anxious Thought.............................	34
A Form of Unbelief...........................	45
As we have Opportunity......................	49
A Pillow-prayer.......HARRIET McEWAN KIMBALL.	51
A Precious Promise...................G. D. M.	53
All in Thee.................................	61
A Gift................................H. W. S.	65
A Good Rule for Travellers.......W. W. L. JAY.	74
A Solemn Thought...........................	80
A Noble Life...............................	98
A Thought for Friends................GOULBURN.	109
Abiding in Christ...........................	127
A Closer Walk..............................	151
Another Day................................	157
Above all, the Shield, HYMNS OF THE CHURCH MILITANT.	202
Avoid Anxiety..............................	219
A Motive for Christian Work.................	231
Being Perplexed............................	23
Be ye Followers of God............GOULBURN.	78
Be Satisfied with Christ.....................	164

Coming Back to Christ.................M'Cheyne. 52
Christ-like..................George Macdonald. 55
Complete in Him..................Anna Warner. 56
Consider one Another. ....Anna Warner. 79
Casting all on Jesus............................. 120
Cheerfulness..................................... 173
Christ, a Refuge......................Bradley. 206
Christ's Service and Ours..................Jukes. 227

Desultory Work........Margaret M. Brewster. 27
Depression............................Whately. 98

Evil Speaking.....................John Wesley. 50
Enter into Thy Closet.....................Cecil. 113
Earthly Care, Heavenly Discipline,
     Harriet Beecher Stowe. 182
Encouragement to Prayer...............Bridges. 194

Full Rest in Jesus.......................R. P. S. 26
Forgetting the Past...........F. W. Robertson. 35
Fellowship with Jesus.........Thomas à Kempis. 92
Far off, yet Near........Anson D. F. Randolph. 162
Faith in the Promises............................ 170
From Self to Christ..............Anna Shipton. 207
Fragments of Time...............Dr. Hamilton. 217
Fresh Springs,
  Author of "The Old, Old Story." 236

Greatly Afflicted.............Nehemiah Adams. 41
God's ways of Answering Prayer.................. 127
Growth in Grace..................Robert Hall. 192

INDEX.

Having Nothing,
    Hymns of the Church Militant. 13
He must Increase, but I Decrease,
      Adelaide Newton. 15
Hope for All.............................Baxter. 34
Harsh Judgments........................Faber. 37
How Shall I Read the Bible..................... 87
Home Trials...................Mrs. Prentiss. 99
He Knoweth our Frame,
    Author of "The Old, Old Story." 140
His Answer.................................... 144
How to Work.......................Goulburn. 148
How to Enter into Rest........................ 158

Inward Trials.................................. 85
In Thy Presence................... Mad. Guyon. 176
In the Field................................... 214
Interruptions in our Work............Goulburn. 190
Jesus the Home of the Solitary....Mrs. Charles. 61
Jesus Only.................................... 168

Looking unto Jesus.....................Staupitz. 39
Life in Christ...............Dora Greenwell. 57
Little Things.......................Goulburn. 117
Love, the Fulfilling of the Law...H. W. Beecher. 145
Life's Drudgeries...................Dr. Deems. 178
Lift up Your Hearts.................Goulburn. 203
Love's Mystery................Miss Sara Start. 203
Lord, Here am I............................... 222
Learning the Lesson...........Dora Greenwell. 233

My Sins and My Saviour......J. B. S. MONSELL. 40
More Light Needed................McCHEYNE. 74
My Shepherd............................M. S. 76
My Need and Thy Love........................ 82
My Debt to Christ.....................BONAR. 91
My Pilgrimage.......................BONAR. 103
Meditation.....................BISHOP HALL. 112
Mental Growth................BALDWIN BROWN. 123

No Choice.................................... 75
Not Lost..................................... 146
No Excuse..........................GURNALL. 187

O God, my Heart is Fixed.........ANNA WARNER. 9
Our Portion.........................BEECHER. 15
One of the Joys of Heaven..............STROUD. 83
Our Single Acre............GEORGE MACDONALD. 95
Oneness with Christ............BALDWIN BROWN. 114
Our Work Held in Everlasting Remembrance,
                                    PRES. WOOLSEY. 126
One Life..............................BONAR. 130
On Helping the Poor..........BALDWIN BROWN. 137
On Religious Conversation ...RANDOM THOUGHTS. 153
On Habit............................GARVEY. 165
Our Privilege................................ 184
Our Earthly Ties................MRS. CHARLES. 187

Promptness in Duty.................MACLEOD. 43
Pillow Prayers............................... 93
Prayer a Service................MRS. CHARLES. 122
Past Troubles................H. W. BEECHER. 134

INDEX.

Quietness in Serving........GEORGE MACDONALD. 77

Rest; Weary Soul.....................PRIDHAM. 95
Read With Prayer...................MELVILLE. 219
Rest in the Lord.............................. 223
Rejoice! Rejoice!............................. 229

Sins Remembered no More....ADELAIDE NEWTON. 24
Sunday a Day of Gladness......RANDOM THOUGHTS 38
Sing Away your Grief...........H. W. BEECHER. 63
Silent Lives.................RANDOM THOUGHTS. 124
Spiritual Weakness............................ 128
Self-knowledge ....TRENCH. 192
Spiritual Depression....................H. W. S. 200
Steps to Holiness......................GOULBURN. 224
Singleness of Purpose......................... 227
St. Paul's Three Psalms of Thanksgiving......... 230

The Knowledge of God................GOULBURN. 7
The Morning Question...........Mrs. CHARLES. 18
The Ministry of Sorrow................G. D. M. 20
The Faith that Moves Mountains................ 21
The Covering of Charity....................... 31
The Sufferer's Couch.........E. H. BICKERSTETH. 44
The Heart of Unbelief.........T. D. CREWDSON. 47
The True Standard.....................HENRY. 60
The Secret Spring,
      AUTHOR of "THE OLD, OLD STORY." 66
The Government of Christ...................... 68
The Fatherhood of God.........H. W. BEECHER. 81
The Secret of Success...................BRIDGES. 89

Trust Him Wholly	H. W. Beecher.	96
The Secret of Edification	Goulburn.	98
Thoughts on Public Worship	Goulburn.	104
The Law of Christ	Mrs. Charles.	105
The Waiting Time	Stopford A. Brooks.	107
The Eternity of God	Faber.	108
The Keeping Power of Christ	Dr. Cullis.	113
The Precious Blood	G. D. M.	131
The Voice of the Blood	C. A. L.	135
True Rest	F. W. Robertson.	136
The Example of our Master	Jukes.	138
The Spirit's Guiding	Goulburn.	142
The Art of Being Miserable	Kingsley.	148
The Thing that I Long For, Author of "The Old, Old Story."		150
The Day a Miniature Life	Goulburn.	156
The Danger of Neglecting Prayer, F. W. Robertson.		166
The Presence of God	Mrs. Charles.	174
The Call		180
The Comforter, which is the Holy Ghost, Hymns of the Spirit.		181
The Burden Laid Down		186
Trust to His Guiding	G. D. M.	195
The Darkness Hideth not from Thee, Anna Warner.		198
The Morning Hour	Goulburn.	199
The Power of the Cross of Christ		211
The Beauty of Holiness	H. W. Beecher.	220
Till He Come	E. H. Bickersteth.	232

INDEX.

Unconscious Influence	MACMILLAN.	63
Unto Thee	BONAR.	171
Unto Him Who Loves us	DR. SCHAFF.	240
Waiting in Faith	ANNA SHIPTON.	11
Wherein we Have Peace		12
What wilt Thou have me to Do		19
What All May Do	RUSKIN.	22
Waiting and Watching for Me		29
Whitefield's Prayer		42
Work for All		48
What Jesus Says to Me		71
Worldly Conformity	ADELAIDE NEWTON.	77
What it is to Abide in Jesus	BOARDMAN.	90
Worldliness		109
Wait on the Lord	KITTO.	160
What He is Able to Do		169
What we Might Have	DORA GREENWELL.	181
Watching unto Prayer	BRIDGES.	210

www.ingramcontent.com/pod-product-compliance
Lightning Source LLC
Chambersburg PA
CBHW020805230426

43666CB00007B/866